GATE H

The Extraordinary Life and Times of a

Prison Governor

Barbara E Treen

ISBN: 9798836803551

Published by Pilosus Publications
www.pilosuspublications.co.uk

0 1 2 3 4 5 6 7 8 9

Overall cover design by: Pilosus Publications
Cover image: www.selfpubbookcovers.com/andrewgraphics

DEDICATION

For Rob, Jennie and Lorna.

CONTENTS

Foreword

I wrote this book primarily to show my children what I was up to all those years when I was 'abandoning them' as they so charitably put it. I also hope, however, to shed a little more light on the mysterious worlds behind the Prison Gate. It is based on 29 years worth of memories. Events may not be quite as others remember but they are as true as I can make them. I am very grateful to the hundreds of colleagues who have supported me throughout my career, my friends and my family. Most names have been changed.

Chapter 1: Recruited

HMP Brockhill, Worcestershire, June 2002

As I cross the carpark, carefully avoiding the rain-filled potholes, I notice a knot of staff surrounding something at the base of the vehicle gate. As I approach, the Senior Officer looks up. "It's Mollie James Ma'am. She's been released but she's refusing to leave. She says there's nothing for her on the outside." I can hear the revving of engines objecting to the delay.

In the grit at our feet, in a foetal position, is a small heap of humanity, screwed up tightly against whatever the future will bring.

This isn't how it was meant to be.

Aberystwyth University, March 1983

I was squashed into a cramped little office on campus one late morning in March. Piles of battered pamphlets covered every surface, leaflets spilling out of cupboards and off shelves. Presiding over this sea of paper was Mr Samuels the Careers Officer, a comfortable man with kind eyes, who didn't trust any new-fangled gizmos.

"Now don't expect too much, we're just trialling it".

Heading for a nondescript degree (with a bit of luck) in Political Science and International Politics I knew that I was fitted for no useful employment. I needed all the help I could get.

The shiny new computer chortled and spluttered out its verdict. To my surprise, my ideal careers apparently were, in order:

Industrial Relations Negotiator
BBC Engineer
NHS Administrator
Security Intelligence Analyst GCHQ
Assistant Governor Her Majesty's Prison Service

When I saw the last entry, a disturbing image of Frodo disappearing through the Gates of Mordor flashed through my mind.

I left the office with plenty of food for thought.

I immediately discounted applying to be an Industrial Relations Negotiator. I don't remember why.

I did not apply to be an Engineer with the BBC. I was proud that my father had taught me to wire a plug, but that was the extent of my talent for things scientific. In a way it was a pity: I would have met my future husband several years earlier than actually occurred.

I did apply to the NHS but they perceptively did not want my services. This may well have been because I wrote what I considered a witty response on the application form, about how I thought the ultimate goal of administration should be to do away with itself. My propensity to think I am being funny at inappropriate times would in the future get me into trouble.

Fancying the idea of travelling the world as a spy clad in shabby gabardine, I applied to GCHQ[1]. Much to my joy they were interested! I hurried off down to Cheltenham to wrestle with a bunch of tests designed to assess one's code breaking ability. It turned out sadly that espionage required a better grip on numbers than I possessed.

_____

[1] Government Communications Headquarters

Ignoring the computer's advice completely, I made one entirely secret trip to London to audition for drama school. I had always harboured a secret passion to act. Unsuccessful, and too crushed to try again, I decided this was another fantasy that had to be firmly put to bed.

I remained less than convinced about the Prison Service. Before this point I'd only encountered the Criminal Justice System through television and books. I thought that I would like to be in a job that helped people, which the Prison Service somewhat surprisingly made quite a big deal about. However, the thought of locking someone up was not very attractive, even if they might really need it. Part of me did like the prospect of trying to outwit dangerous, devious people as that sounded exciting. On the other hand, whenever we played Escape from Colditz in my childhood, I always preferred to be on the side of the POWS. I decided on balance it was worth applying, at least, to see what it was all about.

To become a Trainee Assistant Governor one had to pass a Civil Service Examination. It took place in the Prison Service College, Love Lane, Wakefield. This was a long, low building lying right under the imposing wall of Wakefield Prison. I discovered later that the assessment was commonly known as the 'Country House Test', as it was traditionally the process by which 'Gentlemen Governors' were produced.

I felt that I didn't cover myself with glory. For a start, I don't drink coffee, so exercises where we had to stand around, clinking delicate china while making intelligent conversation, saw me waving my arms around excitedly, while juggling a pint glass of water. Secondly, almost straight away I managed to lose my handbag. After it had been discovered and handed in, I had to retrieve it shame-faced from reception, under the disapproving gaze of the staff. This hardly gave a good first impression of my ability to be 'security aware at all times'. I remember only one positive moment. I informed a Rear Admiral who was interrogating me, that I had survived a stint as a children's camp counsellor in America and had afterwards toured the country on my own, travelling on a succession of Greyhound buses. He glared at me over his half rimmed spectacles, gave a snort, and remarked: "Well that shows a *little* initiative at least!"

Much to my shock a few weeks later a package of papers arrived informing me that I was successful. I had a job! I was delighted and very relieved. I rang my parents, read the contents of the package dozens of times then promptly lost it and had to beg for another one. Security awareness clearly was not my natural forte, and would need to be learned.

That July I graduated from Aberystwyth. My mum and dad travelled up with me for the day and we all stayed in a B&B. They accompanied me to the graduation ceremony. My dad, proud as punch, wore his one, rather faded suit and my mum was uncharacteristically conventionally dressed. Most of the ceremony was in Welsh which I had briefly tried and failed to learn. Then I have an uncomfortable mixed up memory of showing my parents around my old Hall of Residence, Alexandra Hall. I must have left them for a while because I remember returning and as I did so, overhearing someone laughing about a peculiar woman they'd met in the kitchen and the odd things she had said. I knew this was my mother. Of course, I said nothing.

We returned home. My dad took a photograph of me in my rented mortarboard and gown in the parched back garden. I was the first person in the family who had been to university. My mother had briefly been a nurse. My father, the son of an engine driver, had self-educated after being forced into the factory at the bottom of his road. He would have given anything to have had the chance of getting a degree. In the photograph I am standing awkwardly but proud, long brown hair hanging untidily nearly to my waist. I am blinking in the bright sunlight and smiling, looking eagerly forward to the future.

I was due to begin training in the autumn. In the interim I began enthusiastically watching and reading anything I could about prisons. There was *Prisoner Cell Block H* on TV where the walls wobbled, but I didn't find that inspiring. I discovered a battered book in a junk shop containing a few episodes of the TV drama *Within these Walls* starring Googie Withers. I was very impressed. To celebrate, I bought myself a bunch of paisley neck scarves and a 'power suit', thinking that this is what Governors wore. It was an interesting look.

Chapter 2 Fish Out of Water

HMP Brockhill, Worcestershire, May 2002

The brass nameplate on the door says 'Governor'. This is it. Little thrills of excitement and trepidation run up my spine.

My new boss has not exactly gilded the lily about the task ahead: "The prison is falling down, all the women are trying to kill themselves, there are three outstanding inquests, there's no health care centre - there's a multi-million pound scheme to put one in but it looks doubtful it's ever going to happen. Staff sickness has hit the roof, there are major industrial relation issues, you'll be the sixth Governor in four years." He had paused for breath. "Oh and the place is infested with rabbits - most of which have got myxomatosis."

I push open the door ready to meet my management team. Those seated rise as I enter. The first person I notice is Hazel.

Prison Officers' Training School, Wakefield, 1983

I officially joined Her Majesty's Prison Service on the 10th October 1983. I was 21. I was sent to the Officers' Training School at Aberford Road in Wakefield, a modern complex of buildings comprising classrooms, a gym and accommodation on the outskirts of the city.

I was placed into a Section of 22 Trainee Prison Officers including 5 women one of whom was Hazel. Blonde with short spiky hair, very young, quick-witted, Hazel seemed to take to the environment like a fish to water. She would joke and lark around with everyone. Much later I began to suspect underneath she was really quite shy. If she was, she must have found keeping so many other people happy, tiring.

In contrast, I was exceptionally quiet. I wasn't intimidated by being in a mainly male environment. I was, however, deeply afraid of being judged as elitist coming from university and being a Trainee

Assistant Governor - for a time at least 'in disguise'. There were two other Trainee Assistant Governors in my Section I eventually discovered, both women - and we all wanted to 'fit in'.

We felt more of a team as soon as we'd been issued our uniform: shirts that were impossible to keep really clean, soft felt hats resembling those worn by Ken Dodd's 'Diddy Men', that were useless for any function. Very beige tights. Nasty skirts. Women Officers didn't wear trousers in those days. (Much later, I was to be proud when my eldest daughter led a rebellion at her school in a demand to wear trousers). Tough leather belts with a long chain attached to which your keys would be clipped, which "...*must on NO account hit the floor if you drop them!*".

Principal Officer Rudd, our Section Leader, was a very astute short Yorkshire-man with black bushy eyebrows, an excellent trainer with a wicked sense of humour, who worked wonders making half-competent Prison Officers out of some very unpromising material. I liked him a lot.

I only recall snapshots of the training. I know it was mostly practical and enjoyable, very different to the tedious research and essay writing required at university. I was never an enthusiastic academic and had chiefly sought university life as a means of getting away from home.

I have a memory of us all marching in opposite directions like a bunch of drunken beetles, while our Section Leader swore at us. I enjoyed marching. It probably reminded me of my days as a patrol leader in the guides, standing for hours outside our local church for no logical reason, either freezing or baking, proudly holding the company flag. Feeling important.

These were the days when the Prison Service was trying to professionalise the Service, particularly how staff physically 'handled' prisoners. At one point I foolishly escaped while being put in an arm and leg lock on the floor during 'Control and Restraint' training - resulting in several very heavy people instantly and painfully landing on me. I didn't make the same mistake again. In future years, it would be decreed that governor grades should be trained as 'Section Commanders' - to lead Prison Officers into battle in the case of 'concerted indiscipline'[2] by prisoners. On both occasions when my number came up, I managed to avoid it by being pregnant. It wasn't a deliberate ploy but it was probably a good thing. Given my physical ineptitude I would probably have tripped over my shield, fallen flat on my face and been trampled by my colleagues.

We learnt to search cells. We learnt to search people. Later on, somewhat to my surprise, when in Holloway, I was to discover drugs in a prisoner's boots and spotted some hidden in a wall duct, and felt very pleased with myself. Searching is one of the few Prison Officer skills that has benefited me all my life, particularly in a family that regularly loses everything.

---

2 'Concerted Indiscipline' is the term used when two or more prisoners act together to break prison rules. It is commonly used to describe prison protests or riots.

It soon became known that some of us were Trainee Assistant Governors. It wasn't an issue for most people but it seemed to affect a few. I found a couple of the women Trainee Prison Officers positively scary. They weren't bad people but they were loud, worldly-wise and their language felt intimidating to me. My parents didn't swear much and neither did my university circle. The women would tease me sometimes about being 'different' in a rather savage way. Listening to my mother's rages when small had made me uneasy around aggressive women and it would be a while until I could confidently manage encounters like these. It didn't help that they left me in no doubt that they saw me as a complete twit. I was genuinely touched though, when one of them, Angela, after an impromptu concert at which I was roped in to play bad guitar, pulled me aside: "I didn't think you'd do that", she said, "Coming from Roedean."

Angela had assumed that because I had a southern (Brighton) accent I must be a snob and have gone to private school. My lack of effort in getting to know her hadn't helped improve my image of course. Her opinion of me however, had now gone up. She hadn't been dazzled by my musical ability (no one would be) but she had been impressed by my attempt to muck in and make a fool of myself.

I don't really like socialising, particularly with people I don't know well. I would much rather spend my down-time alone, preferably with a book in the bath. By the end of the course however, I had grown quite close to some of the older men. They welcomed me into their little group and I was completely at ease. We talked about home, family and hobbies. Eddie was large, had red cheeks, a wide grin and an impressive handlebar moustache. He used to drive us to a pub a few miles out of Wakefield where the group attempted to teach me pool. I even found myself sufficiently at ease one night to venture out with them to Casanova's Nightclub in Wakefield, for a fancy dress competition. My costume? A catsuit. My tail fell off and I won a bottle of Champagne.

Then the course was at an end. We had a celebratory dinner, a parade, and I said some fond goodbyes. The real challenges were about to begin.

Chapter 3: The Finishing School

HMP Brockhill, Worcestershire, Spring 2002

You hear the code words over the radio summoning nursing staff urgently to the scene and your stomach hits the floor. The prison stands still for a second holding its breath. Everyone's thoughts are with the woman and the staff fighting to save her. Then people carry on with the daily routine. Subdued. Hurting. Hoping. You're in charge: you have things to do. You don't need to but you phone the Gate and tell them to stand by to admit emergency vehicles with no delay. You artificially slow down your voice: staff are relying on you to be calm. Your hand is shaking slightly: adrenaline is kicking in. You make sure there are staff on the scene to relieve those attempting resuscitation. Soon, hopefully, you hear the sirens. You ring round checking that the rest of the prison is OK. Then, when it is finally clear that hope is lost, you pull out contingency plans. You ring more people: the Incident Management Unit, the Independent Monitoring Board, the Chaplain, the Area Manager. You check there is a doctor on the way in, to certify death. You contact the police to confirm that they will break the news to the next of kin. You check again on the rest of the prison, especially those at most risk. You make sure people are being debriefed, a quick 'hot' debrief for those involved before they go off duty. Later you will arrange 'cold' debriefs for longer analysis. You talk and you listen and you listen and you listen. And you reassure everyone that they have done everything they could possibly have done. And you begin assembling the mass of evidence that you will need to present to the Police, the Coroner, the Ombudsman.

I thought Holloway had prepared me for this but I was wrong.

HMP Holloway, London, 1983-1984

Holloway, originally built in 1852, was the largest women's prison in the country when I joined the Prison Service, holding just over 500 women. Many notorious individuals had been incarcerated within its walls and it had earned a grim reputation. Occasionally I heard Holloway sarcastically referred to by its inhabitants as 'the Finishing School'. It was certainly seen as the end of the road for many.

My introduction to the prison was mortifying, thanks to my sweet but sometimes embarrassing father. He had driven me up that morning from Brighton in our lurid green Ford Escort. The imposing front wall of the prison was red brick. Within it rose an enormous brown wooden vehicle gate. We approached this slowly and stopped. A smartly dressed Officer Support Grade[3] appeared out of the pedestrian entrance and walked up to the car. I was nervous, keen to make a good impression. Then dad, peering over the top of his thick black spectacles, leaned out of the car window and demanded earnestly: "My daughter's starting here - she's got all this luggage. Can she bring it all with her or should I take some back?"

So, red-face, I had arrived at Holloway. I noticed as we parked the car in the car park, round the side of the wall, that there were a lot of workmen around. Later I was to discover that the final bricks of the 'new' Holloway were just being laid.

---

3 A uniformed member of staff who assists with the running of the prison but usually does not supervise prisoners.

If you ask anyone who has ever worked at Holloway what the major problem with the place was, I can guarantee you that they will all tell you the same thing: "The Design"

When I arrived the 'new' Holloway had only been around for six years. Later I came to read the architect's vision. It was to be a 'secure hospital', not a prison. The concept was a disaster. It is true that the majority of women prisoners have mental health issues and many are intensely vulnerable. Trying to build a prison while attempting to disguise the fact that it's a prison however, simply does not work.

Galleried landings were abandoned in favour of multiple small units with right angle bends in the corridors. Sightlines were only a few metres meaning you were always out of view of your colleagues. Prisoners and staff felt isolated and often unsafe. As a consequence of the design the place needed very high levels of people to run it. I didn't know the difference as I had never worked in the old Holloway but for those who had, the glorious dream of an efficient, purpose-built, modern building must have been a sorry disappointment. To complete the monstrosity, the perimeter wall surrounding the prison was now snake-like, again presumably, in an attempt to disguise what it was. You couldn't see along it for more than about fifty metres because of the curves. Everyone called it 'the wibbly wobbly wall'. The Victorians knew a thing or two. No one before or since has beaten the design of the radial, galleried prison, and even now the best modern penal designs are modifications of it.

After saying a rather hasty goodbye to my dad and signing in that first morning I dragged ALL of my luggage round the prison wall into my newly allocated Prison Officer quarter. 'Quarters' were houses or flats owned by the Prison Service and rented to staff. Holloway quarters were split level flats with a shared kitchen and bathroom, located round the back of the prison and far too close to it. You could even see right into one of the prison wings when you were washing your smalls in the laundry. Psychologically, it wasn't healthy. Staff need some distance from what is often a very stressful and intense job.

My flat-mate's name, it appeared, was Mandy and she would scare the bejeezus out of me. I am an only child, a confirmed introvert and I accept that I don't share space terribly well but this situation would have tested a saint. Whoever paired us up clearly wanted to see how long I lasted. Mandy was very aggressive and very inquisitive. She seemed fascinated by this weird specimen who had been dumped on her and to my horror would interrogate me about whatever I was up to, whenever she could corner me.

She was also extremely loud. When 'Relax' by Frankie Goes to Hollywood was in the charts, Mandy played it on continuous loop, at maximum volume, night and day. With strange irony this was to become one of my youngest daughter's favourite tracks many moons later, but at the time it drove me insane.

I quite admired her ability to form relationships though (my love life was non-existent) and a series of boyfriends would visit the flat. But I didn't think they made her very happy. She had an ashtray shaped in the form of male genitalia she used to viciously stub her cigarettes out on.

One thing that particularly intrigued me about Mandy was that she would regularly dye her hair in many and varied colours (which was novel then) and the Chief Officers let her get away with it. Perhaps she scared the bejeezus out of them too.

Years later I met some staff from Holloway and mentioned Mandy. They said she'd been sacked after stabbing someone in the Prison Officers' club.

Having survived my initial encounter with my new flatmate that first night, however, I escaped to my room. My new uniform, neatly pressed, hung in the wardrobe opposite me. I lay on the bed watching out of my window the shimmering lights of the prison, wondering what the next morning would bring. I felt excited, desperate to learn and determined not to be a completely cack-handed useless graduate. I knew it wasn't going to be easy.

A prison is a total institution and a community. It is an enclosed system where all its inhabitants live and work together according to rules that often seem strange to those on the outside.

Holloway mostly held women 'on remand'. This means they are awaiting trial and have not been convicted of any crime. On days they were due to attend court they would be woken early, given a nominal breakfast in their rooms, then escorted bleary eyed and dressed in their best, out of the prison.

Around 7.30am the new shift of staff would arrive and the prison roll would be taken. This count confirms the handover between night and day staff of the correct number of prisoners. Alive. Then chatter, washing and dressing. Breakfast for those that bothered. An endless queue for medications and call ups to see the doctor. Women would then leave for classes, work, visits with solicitors and the wings would become briefly deserted.

At 11.30am there would be a rush of noise as women returned for lunch. There were small dining rooms at Holloway but most chose to eat in their rooms with people they had begun to trust. Lockdown over lunch. If there was no one at risk to check on, the patrolling Officer would put her feet up in the office and read the papers. Women dozed or listened to radios in their rooms, when they could afford them. At this point there were no TVs in cells[4].

After lunch for the lucky few: visits with friends or family. They usually returned quickly. Visits for someone on remand lasted a minimum of 15 minutes, and at busy times that's all prisoners got. It was hard for small children to understand why they had to leave their mothers so soon. A few others went off to work around the prison or to the

---

4 TVs in cells were introduced in 1995 partly to improve the regime but mainly as a means of control. It is easier to lock people up for longer if you have a device to occupy them. Prisoners have to pay a weekly fee to have a TV in their cells and it can be removed as a punishment if they misbehave.

large gym for PE. The rest stayed locked up or would clean the wing except for a minimum of one hour a day when exercise was taken on the large yard. Women would wander aimlessly around, arms linked, passing the time of day, or sometimes, a little bit of something they shouldn't, to help them get through.

Tea was very early. If there were enough staff on the evening shift, women were allowed out 'on association' to mingle and chat or watch the wing TV. If they were 'on association' they had easier access to the pay phones and baths, otherwise staff had to let them out one by one. Then women newly sentenced or remanded, or returning part way through court proceedings, would start flooding in.

At around 8.45pm night staff would arrive and the roll would again be taken. Lights were switched off early and the wings would quickly quieten down. Peace. Then various disturbances would begin around the prison. Someone would argue in her sleep - a nightmare. A plea from a woman for pain killers. Occasionally a cell would have to be opened up to check on a prisoner at risk. Then quiet would resume again until the morning. And so each day would repeat while prisoners streamed in and out of the system: a relentless, broken, tide.

I soon picked up that few of these women were hardened criminals. Far less women commit crime and end up in prison than men, and men generally commit more serious offences. A woman will inevitably arrive however, with a raft of other problems including substance misuse and mental health issues. Around half of all women prisoners will have experienced violence and a third of them will have been victims of sexual abuse - mostly inflicted by men.

I walked into the prison from a position of privilege. There had always been food on the table and a roof over my head. I had enjoyed a good education and my home, although not very happy, was physically safe. The women I locked up were in a very different situation.

In my early days at Holloway I met Anna who had been arrested just that morning. She was thin and cold and her hair was in rats-tails. Many of her teeth were missing. I supplied her with a flannel, plain soap and tooth powder. Toothpaste was too expensive for the prison to provide. She looked about 40 but she was probably half that. Women prisoners are allowed to wear their own clothing but she didn't have any family who could send fresh clothes in. She would be dependent on the charity box. I found her some spare underwear, a grey t-shirt and jogging bottoms. All were far too big. She wouldn't need sanitary protection. Drug misuse and underfeeding had stopped her periods long ago.

Many women were in the same state as Anna when they entered prison, but a few weren't. These were the days of the Greenham Common protests and van-loads of women would arrive regularly: some loud and cheering, keeping each other's spirits up, a few scared but being brave. They weren't very popular among the rest of the prisoners. They weren't seen as their 'kind'.

We had our occasional notable prisoner too. Sarah Tisdall was one. Her cell was full of flowers. They had been arriving continuously from well wishers since she had been sentenced to 6 months in prison for breaking the Official Secrets Act. She had supplied the Guardian newspaper with details of when American nuclear cruise missiles would be arriving in Britain, information that she had discovered while working as a Clerical Officer in the Foreign and Commonwealth Office. She was being rationed now to three bunches a day, the rest of her flowers remaining at the Gate. She had readily agreed that the processing of other prisoners' incoming goods should take priority.

Many of the women were suffering with serious mental health issues. The most distressed were located on the lowest landing 'C1', where nursing staff as well as the most experienced Officers were based. This wing of the bewildered and unfortunate was referred to by some as the 'Muppet Wing'. It was a term of abuse and derision voiced by those that feared mental illness. To try and reduce the women's isolation, cell hatches were left down and we were warned to walk along the very centre of the landing in case the most disturbed prisoners grabbed us through them.

Distress was everywhere. I became used to seeing Officers racing into cells to remove ligatures, women with arms and legs laced with scars, once a cell literally flooded with blood. After a while it wasn't shocking any more.

Self injury is a coping mechanism, very common in all groups and classes in society and is not usually an attempt at suicide. People who self-injure may talk about the need to punish themselves, to control their bodies when they can control nothing else, or to feel 'alive' or 'real'. Often those who self-injure have experienced sexual or other abuse. Sometimes self-injury can become

addictive: stopping the hab
crack than breaking an ad
self-injury was understoo
today.

Nowadays the policy ს.
wherever possible, to manage prisoners w...
injure 'normally', with only very brief periods during
a crisis, of increased supervision, and perhaps the
temporary removal of items someone might use to
harm themselves. At Holloway at that time, there
was a much harsher approach. If a women was
deemed to be at immediate risk of suicide she
would be watched constantly by Prison Officers
sitting in shifts outside her cell - but you cannot
watch every single prisoner at risk around the
clock. So many women, particularly the 'regular
self-harmers' found themselves for days on end in
tear-proof canvas dresses and shorts, tied on with
plastic ties, underwear removed in case they tried
to suffocate or strangle themselves with it,
confined in stripped out cells on a bare stone
plinth covered with a tough canvas mattress and

their mood of course was unlikely to e under such a regime.

Not that placing someone in these harsh conditions stops someone from self-injuring if they are determined to do so. Desperation just forces people to be more creative.

Two severe acts of self-harm stay in my mind. I came on duty one morning to find a woman had been taken to hospital after trying to cut out one of her eyes. I knew who she was as I had met her on C1 wing a few days earlier. A few weeks later a woman attempted to cut off one of her breasts. I noticed her in passing, shortly after her return, bandaged up and sitting in her cell talking calmly to a nurse. The woman who had lost one of her eyes I actually met later when I visited Broadmoor as part of my governor's training, she was cheerfully cutting out material in a handiwork class. I was impressed that she was trusted now with scissors and glad that she seemed to be in a better environment.

Sometimes evening duty staff would be grateful if there were staff shortages and it meant the wings had to be locked up, because they felt their evening would be easier. The women would not be out making demands, or annoying each other which sometimes led to fights. I understood that; the days were long and wearing for staff but the view was short-sighted. The women's mental health was the worse for isolation and instances of self-injury would escalate.

Sometimes I found my responsibilities supervising such troubled people beyond reason. Just before the start of one night duty, during the handover, I was casually warned about a heavily pregnant prisoner who was rhythmically pacing up and down in her room.

"Call Control straightaway if it looks like she's going into labour," I was instructed. "She's said she's going to kill the baby as soon as it's born. We have to get in and grab it."

The prisoner never spoke a word that night, she just kept pacing, until in the early hours of the morning, she suddenly lay down and appeared to fall asleep. I didn't budge from my post, spending most of that shift outside her door peering through the observation slit, barely daring to blink. I never found out the woman's background or what furies were tormenting her mind.

Unsurprisingly, unlike Hazel who had returned to Holloway with me and was proving an excellent Prison Officer, I was pretty hopeless at the job. I was very willing, but I made mistakes and I was, as expected, a bit of a clutz. I once picked up a group of women to escort them to various clinics around the gaol and managed to leave one locked in a stairwell for some considerable time. Luckily for me, if a pity for the poor woman, this probably wasn't unusual and I don't think she noticed.

My major faux pas however, was the Key Compromise Incident. This is one of the major nightmares of any Prison Governor. If keys get into the wrong hands it can result in serious security breaches and the whole of the prison having to be 're-locked' costing thousands, potentially millions of pounds. And probably the loss of one's career. I didn't cause the prison to be relocked but I did merrily leave a London Crown Court with all their cell keys. I discovered them in my pocket as soon as I walked back into Holloway, confessing to staff at the Gate. They went into a whispered huddle, urgent calls were made and somehow court staff miraculously appeared within the hour and smuggled the keys back. I assume what I had done was never reported by Gate staff to the Governor as I was never summoned to be told my fortune. When I realised eventually that they had covered up for me I was touched. I may have been an Assistant Governor in disguise but Officers accepted me as a comrade in arms.

It was important to me to feel that I was a part of the Prison Officer team. Even though I was a Trainee Assistant Governor I joined the Prison Officers Association while I was at Holloway - surprising the Chairperson. I just felt it was right. I've always believed in solidarity, sticking together for what you believe in - " together we're stronger" (or "together we're stranger" as my daughters used to say). I remember being in one POA branch meeting in the Holloway chapel and making a point forcibly against the management point of view, about some HQ initiative being discussed.

Holloway's chief purpose as a Local Prison was to serve the courts and the whole regime revolved around this. Each day around 10-30 Prison Officers were involved in escorting women all over London and the surrounding counties.

We dropped women off at Magistrates courts where the police would look after them before they were either bailed or remanded back into custody. We could travel many miles for these 'drop offs' and the journey back was always fun as we had no prisoner to worry about.

We would also escort women to local Crown Courts for trial. Prison Officers from the male prisons were in overall control of cell areas in these courts but we stayed with our women, looking after them in the cells, sitting with them in the dock and accompanying them back to the prison each night. Sometimes trials could go on for weeks before women learned their fate.

An escort to court and a long 'day out' was considered a nice number by most staff. When I joined it was just before 'Fresh Start' a radical overhaul of the working conditions of the Prison Service when overtime would be eradicated. Before that, it was the 'done thing' not to return from escorts too early or you would lose money, so people generally strung things out. Two young Officers sadly informed me that they were now in the dog-house with their peers after returning from one court rather too early, thereby revealing that the job could be done much quicker.

I quite liked court duties, apart from fraud trials. To sit in the dock for a whole day without falling asleep, whilst also not understanding a word, was a major challenge. Once I was so bored I snuck in a small handheld video game (they were just coming in then) and played it under the edge of the dock. But I was only brave (or stupid) enough to do that once.

Although a day out for us was often light relief from the gaol, it was anything but for the women of course. One collapsed in my arms after receiving a lengthy sentence at Snaresbrook Crown Court. It seemed a long way back to the court cells, through endless cold concrete corridors, half carrying the sobbing woman.

Despite the difficult days and the horrible things we sometimes had to deal with, there were enjoyable times. Picking up ice creams in a pixie (a little green police van) on Brighton seafront, having dropped off a prisoner, laughing with fellow Officers on the way back to London. Telling someone, to their great amusement, that I was sure that there were prisoners sitting in the training block outside the gate, only to discover it was the cast of Prisoner Cell Block H on a visit. The best tasting pizza I have ever had, bought on Upper

Street Islington, and eaten on the Mother and Baby Unit at 2am one morning.

I was often detailed to work on the Mother and Baby Unit. Prison Service 'MBUs' are unique places. The unit at Holloway held mothers with babies under nine months of age, other units catering for those up to eighteen months. A woman is carefully assessed to determine whether she is of minimum risk to the public and a fit parent before being allowed to have her baby with her in an MBU. (This begs the question of course, why most women need to be in MBUs and can't instead, be held on bail if unconvicted, or be allowed to serve their sentences in the community). Women look after their babies during the evenings and nights and may go to work elsewhere within the gaol during the day while their babies are cared for by nursery nurses on the unit.

Mother and Baby Units were little bright spots of colour and clatter but I always detected an air of sadness, of anticipated loss. The prisoner serving a long sentence who finally needed to say goodbye. And the worried woman who projected her own fear onto her baby: "I've decided to hand him out. He knows he's in prison. He's not happy".

Mothers were located in single rooms on this unit and each contained a cot for the baby (or babies - one of our women had twins). There were also small dormitories containing heavily pregnant women. It was a rather odd rule that although mothers were locked within the wing (and of course within the walls of the prison), it was not the done thing to lock a baby within a prisoner's room, so these were left unlocked at night. Women were on their honour not to leave their rooms except in an emergency and I never knew them to break this rule.

The Mother and Baby Unit at Holloway was responsible for my only 'supernatural' experience in the Prison Service.

Holloway, like most gaols, had a reputation for having its share of ghosts. I've never been scared of the supernatural but the place was undeniably eerie at night. The prison had existed for over 130 years. It wasn't hard to imagine, out of all the thousands of sad and frightened souls who had lived and died in that troubled place, how a few might still walk its corridors unable to rest.

When on night duty, Officers were required to regularly patrol the landings, checking on any prisoner who rang their bell or was on any kind of 'watch' (usually because they were at risk of self-injury or suicide). In order to prove you were still awake and to some degree alert, you had to insert a 'peg' into various 'pegging clocks'. These were small mechanical devices looking rather like those toddler shape sorters, attached to the wall at various points around the unit.

I was patrolling the darkened Mother and Baby Unit and adjacent wing one night, regularly 'pegging', when, about three hours into my shift, a cell bell rang. I was on the Mother and Baby Unit at the time and the bell was ringing from a cell at the very end of the next wing. I crept off to investigate, torch in hand, as usual wearing soft shoes so as not to wake the prisoners. It was quite a trek to get there. On arrival I peered through the observation slit to make out the dim shapes of women in their beds. I turned the cell bell off and waited outside for a while, listening. Nothing, just a sigh as a woman turned in her sleep.

At that moment a cell bell rang back on the Mother and Baby Unit. I trekked back there and discovered exactly the same situation: the pregnant women in the dormitory where the bell had rung all appeared fast asleep. As I turned the cell bell off a bell erupted again on the other wing. I walked back there more quickly now and found once again, nothing amiss. The torch cast strange shadows on the way back to the office.

It is possible that this was a pre-arranged and very well organised ruse set up by prisoners on two different wings to worry a gullible Prison Officer. It is possible the top bunks in the different rooms were positioned too near the cell bells and occupied co-incidentally by women who thrashed around in their sleep and kicked them. Or perhaps it was a restless spirit or two having some fun. Whatever the cause, it was a creepy incident and freaked me out for the rest of the night.

Most of my shifts were not that exciting. As a newbie I spent much of my time escorting women to and fro the meandering corridors of Holloway: to 'Special' (VD) clinics, to visits, the dentist, the doctor or I ran errands for supplies. When permitted to stand still I would supervise prisoners on association or while cleaning and chat with them. The days were long, sometimes tedious and often my feet ached. To sit down in the office was a bit of a treat. The more senior you were, the more chance you had of getting a chair.

As time went by I became better at talking to, and more importantly listening to, prisoners. Wherever you went women just wanted to talk. It is a great truth that if you ask a male prisoner: "How are you?" he will generally appreciate the inquiry and you will get a brief "OK Guv". If you ask a woman prisoner however, be prepared, because she will tell you her life story, and you'll need time to listen.

I've often been asked if I was ever in a situation when I felt in danger in my career. The answer is only a handful of times. Neither did I ever really worry that I would be tracked down by an angry prisoner outside. It could happen of course. A Governor I knew received a threatening letter at his home address, from an IRA prisoner. In later years I did make sure that when my children's photos were occasionally in the local paper after some excitement at school, their surnames were not published.

The only time I (knowingly) encountered a prisoner outside, was on Eastbourne seafront one Summer. Casually enjoying a walk through the town, a rather scruffy man in his late 50s suddenly streaked up the road and wrapped his arms around me in a bear hug. It was a lifer I had been responsible for, now out on licence. Then overcome with embarrassment at his impetuosity, he briefly greeted me and hurriedly walked off. I was glad to see he was doing well.

I never felt personally at risk by a woman prisoner. That's not to say all women prisoners were shrinking violets. Many put up a tough front, enough for others to leave them alone. Some would get into fights with their peers or staff after sensing (or imagining) injustice or disrespect. A few could be extremely violent. Usually these women would have serious mental health conditions. Most of the women that got into trouble were, I think, underneath, scared and defensive, even if they had been in prison many times.

I was never personally involved in any violent incidents at Holloway except once, when I foolishly managed to get between two women having a tiff and received the full force of a vase of rancid flowers and water. In male prisons then, the assault of choice was 'potting' (the hurling of a full chamber pot) so I got off lightly. The new Holloway luckily had integral sanitation[5]. This was one of the

---

5 Toilets installed within cells.

few times I have had to place a prisoner 'on report'.

When prisoners commit offences against prison rules they are 'put on report' by staff and sent before a governor for 'adjudication'. This is similar to a short court process. If found guilty prisoners could be punished in a number of ways from having a day's pay stopped to having additional days added to their sentences. It was quite intimidating the first time giving evidence in the segregation unit, in front of the Deputy Governor, the now sanguine prisoners and accompanying Officers.

I gradually got to know more of the Holloway staff. A couple of individuals were dour and short with the women and you wondered why they had joined when they seemed to hate the work. Or maybe they had grown to hate it? Most Officers however, could definitely be described as 'firm but fair'. You could see they understood the women's vulnerabilities and did their best for them. One though, plainly adored her job. Miss Alda was a very tall, thin Officer with distinctive features who on first sight would appear to be everyone's stereotype of a terrifying 'warder'. But she was the sweetest woman and universally loved by both staff and prisoners.

There were however, a couple of staff cliques which felt toxic to me and I became very mouse-like when members of those were on duty. I was warned not to go into the Prison Officers Club in fact, as one of the cliques apparently 'ruled' the place and 'they' were 'trouble'. In the years following my departure there were major investigations following allegations by some junior Officers of systematic and brutal bullying. After one, the then Director General Martin Narey stated: "staff who have been there some time effectively established themselves as an alternative management structure."

In the short time I was at Holloway even I could sense there was a leadership problem: few senior or middle managers seemed to be respected by anyone. The Deputy Governor and the Assistant Governors seemed pleasant but were distant. I never met them on the landings. The two Chief Officers were feared and one was said to have a major problem with alcohol. The Principal and Senior Officers were openly mocked as soon as they left the offices - and not in an affectionate way. And many of the senior staff were malicious about each other, in front of us, their juniors.

The 'No. 1 Governor' (or 'Governing Governor') was in charge and responsible for the management and health of the establishment. This is the person that I aspired to be. I met the Governing Governor of Holloway only once, the formidable Miss Joy Kinsey, and that was not in ideal circumstances. Having finally escaped from my interesting flatmate, I had found somewhere else to live. I was taken to a party by my new flat-mate where everyone was smoking weed. Having led a very law-abiding existence at university and a very narrow life at home, this wasn't an environment I was comfortable in and I was extremely worried. I couldn't easily leave as I had been given a lift and I was so paranoid about getting sacked, should somehow it be discovered that I had been present at this den of iniquity (goodness knows how) I went and confessed the next day to the Governor. She sat there, formidable, and silent behind her impressive desk, as I grovelled before her, then barked out: "Do YOU take cannabis?" Flustered, I assured her I didn't. She pointed to the door. That was our sole conversation. The day of the approachable Governing Governor, who would be out regularly walking the landings, trying their best to get to know and lead staff, was yet to come.

Lack of leadership has effects. Standards weren't enforced, sickness was high and neglect was obvious. The impossible building with its endless corridors didn't help the battle to keep the place clean. Cockroaches were endemic: they would swarm up the outside of the prison at night. They worked their way inside too.

"Don't stamp on them", I was earnestly and sinisterly warned, "it spreads the eggs".

Eventually my time at Holloway drew to a close. Before officially moving on, I was sent on two short secondments. One was a few days at a psychiatric hospital. There I realised that prisons and the NHS had a fundamentally different approach to looking after the vulnerable people in their care. Doctors in that hospital quickly used drugs, often without consent, to relieve their patients' suffering. In contrast, doctors in Holloway, as far as I knew, never administered drugs to prisoners without consent. In contrast, prisoners suffering mental distress that health care staff were unable to get transferred out to psychiatric services, would be confined and often end up physically restrained by staff.[6] The hospital I visited co-incidentally, was the one where my mother had been a patient and

<hr>

6 There were padded cells, leather belts and cuffs and straight-jackets still in occasional use in prisons too in those days, although not at Holloway.

undergone ECT[7], when I was seven years old. I remembered visiting her and feeding the squirrels.

My second secondment was a month working with Brighton Probation Service. I spent time with staff, visiting clients in their homes, writing reports and attending court. I even went rock climbing with some probation volunteers and their clients. There's nothing like dangling on a rope, twelve metres up in the air, at the mercy of someone you barely know, to encourage you to build up trust.

One night I accompanied an older Probation Officer Mrs Chester, as she distributed food to the homeless under the Palace Pier. She was due for retirement that year. The soup run was not part of her job and she knew everyone by name. A fundamental change was beginning at this time. Probation staff were no longer meant to be 'befriending' those they worked with - they were to be sentence 'enforcers'. There was fear in the air that something very valuable was soon to be lost.

---

7 Electroconvulsive therapy, previously known as Electric Shock therapy involves electrically caused seizures to the brain and has been used to treat illnesses like depression.

My mentor arranged for me to spend a night with Brighton Police. Once upon a time I had wanted to be a Police Officer but my eyesight had sadly ruled that out (these were the days before laser eye surgery) so this was a thrill. Myself, a Sergeant and a dog handler were the entire police response team for the whole of Brighton and Hove that night.

An alarm went off on the Palace Pier. We raced down there, blue lights flashing and sirens wailing. It was exciting searching the Pier by torchlight, you could see the dark water swooshing wildly underneath through the gaps in the planks. Then a 999 call. A burglary was underway in a residential property above Churchill Square. We high-tailed it up there to find a smashed-in door and the 'perps' still inside. The dog handler threw the dog in and shut the door.

"He'll sort them out", He said.

Afterwards I was told we had one more urgent call to make. We drove around the corner where the owner of the cops' favourite chip shop presented us with all his unsold wares.

That was an excellent night.

Chapter 4: The Gentlemen's Club

HMP Brockhill, Worcestershire, 2002

I know the theory. I am going to be a true consultative leader. I hit the ground running. I spend hours walking the landings, talking to staff and prisoners. I'm lucky the place is small - it doesn't take long to get around! I hold full staff meetings and chair discussion groups assessing our strengths and weaknesses, what we want to achieve and how we are going to get there.

My one ambition has been to govern my own prison. The wave of pleasure I have marching around Brockhill and realising what I have accomplished is brief.

Love Lane Training College, Wakefield, 1984-1986

I arrived back at Wakefield for the start of our two-year Assistant Governors 'sandwich' course feeling a little wiser having completed my stint at Holloway. I was 22. I was joined by a cohort of 29 colleagues ranging from a handful of other 'under 24s' who had survived the best part of a year as a Prison Officer and others, who being older, had only been required to complete three months. A wide range of former professions were represented, for example: a male nurse, an artist, a soldier and a pub manager.

It didn't take me long to realise that I was among some of the cleverest, funniest people I'd ever meet, and a few of the laziest and most dodgy too. These were to be the future leaders of the Prison Service.

By the end of the two year course, two of our members had disappeared. Shockingly, quiet Aiden, the only ex-Prison Officer on our course, simply didn't arrive back one week. He had been arrested following numerous allegations of 'sexual misconduct in a public place'. Almost as startlingly, quirky Leigh, who had very long dark hair and was the course's resident hippie, vanished after a particular edition of 'Reader's Wives' circulated at her young offender institution.

In the cohort also was the future Director General of the Prison Service, Michael Spurr, already displaying his customary modesty and brains.

Wisely he went home at weekends and avoided the worst of the shenanigans.

This motley crew was led by a pair of tutors, one man, one woman. Equally bright, they were excellent teachers: wise, witty and very entertaining. Alice was excellent but I didn't know her very well as I wasn't in her set. I thought of my tutor as 'Mr Machismo'. He was charming and charismatic. I admired his abilities, enjoyed being taught by him and wanted to impress him, but found him quite intimidating.

Beneath the capable exterior there was a different side. He would have affairs with some of the female students on the courses he taught. It sometimes made for rather an uncomfortable atmosphere.

I found quite a lot of the course fun. One week we practised our presentation skills. Naturally I delivered a long and (to me) fascinating account of the history of theatre (with diagrams) from ancient

Greece to the modern day. My friend Judith gave an erudite talk about the Coriolis effect. Clarence, (who went on to a very senior career), inspired by Michael Bond's The Herbs childrens' TV series, acted out with shuddering sobs and mournful gestures the sad history of how Parsley the Lion lost his tail. I don't know why Clarence decided to tell the story and to this day I don't understand why he had to be hoisted up the tree to enable his tail to re-grow (the lion, not Clarence). Perhaps it's because I'm not a gardener.

Tom gave an enthusiastic and well informed exposition of the history of the Yanomami tribe in the Amazonian rainforest. He described all the rich life the forest had to offer, and gave an authentic imitation of some of the tribe's calls. His talk attracted ear-splitting and enthusiastic audience participation. Tom was a very intelligent man, but so eccentric that he was apparently made to stand in the centre of his prison wing for all three months' of his training, his supervising Senior Officer barking at him: "On NO account are you to move!" Tom was to go on to govern his own prison, but tragically not for long. He was to die in a car accident not many years later.

Sometimes I still felt like a 'fish out of water' and something of an innocent in this crazy, mostly older, and much more worldly-wise gang. I didn't go to the pubs or nightclubs with the others in the evenings and hung around with Judith for mutual support. Not that she needed it. Judith appeared even younger than me, being elfin in stature, with enormous blue eyes, a mass of blonde hair and a merry laugh. The girlish exterior however, masked a steely interior. She had been a high academic achiever all her life and was very independent. I would always be a little jealous of her confidence and determination.

We learned quite a lot on our course although what we gleaned is rather hard to quantify. We had long erudite conversations. Our confidence grew. We did learn something about prison rules, the criminal justice system and what we were trying to achieve. We gained some practical skills like how to check sentence calculations (then a requirement for Governors) and how to conduct adjudications. At the end we probably thought we knew a great deal more than we did. I found much of it interesting and I was rarely bored.

Occasionally our tutors would unwisely invite outsiders in to try to teach us something. One of them lectured us on personal autonomy and foolishly announced: "You have the power to make your own choices - and we want to encourage you to do that - to exercise your independence". So we took him at his word and went off to play Monopoly all afternoon until Alice dragged us back.

The fact is that by the end of the two years we were pretty much unteachable. Not many of us would admit to being fond of each other, but when irritated by outsiders we could round on them like a pack of velociraptors.

Towards the end of the course we had a farewell party. Leo, who never appeared to age, performed a poem he had written about all of our idiosyncrasies. Very rude and very accurate. He would become a respected and forever youthful Area Manager.

The last days of our course coincided with major industrial unrest in the prisons. We were hauled in front of the course Director to be told the latest news. Following the threat of industrial action, the Governor of Gloucester prison had decided to bar most of his staff from the gaol. (He apparently deployed some enterprising trickery involving a delivery of fish and chips to gain control of the Gate). Governors were being dispatched from all across the country to help him.

The programme Director rose to his feet. "Don't worry", he reassured us, peering over the top of his spectacles, "I've been told categorically that on no account will any of you be sent as you are still under training". Twenty minutes later we were on the motorway.

I found myself being driven hell for leather down the M1 in Rowan's nice red sports car. I felt exhilarated - we were racing to the rescue of our colleagues in their time of need! Less dramatically, our desperate mission paused briefly as, in convoy, we streamed into a service station for a very civilised tea and scones (well we were graduates of the Gentlemen's Club), before zooming off again.

My adrenaline was still pumping as we arrived at Gloucester prison. A small group of people were milling around outside the gate and there was tension in the air. I felt very self-conscious. Someone took photographs of us. There was a police presence. I noticed a few of the excluded staff staring at us, shuffling their feet, looking grim.

This wasn't the last time we would be sent as 'cannon fodder' as someone cynically called it, when staff had walked out (or in this case been tricked out by means of fast food). We didn't have much choice, of course. Regardless of duty and our (unwritten) conditions of service, prisoners had to be cared for and protected from themselves and others. I understood my duty but I never felt comfortable about what I was being asked to do.

I and the rest of the women in our group were initially deposited in the 'Chief Officer's Clerk's Office' to censor the mail (checking that nothing illegal was being smuggled in). The enterprising Governing Governor however, then had the bright idea of putting us on the landings to supervise prisoners. This would have been a first for women staff at that time and he was going to do it. We marched onto the wing eager to take this historic step. Men were out of their cells; I could feel their eyes on us. The experiment didn't last long. A note appeared almost instantly in the wing mailbox:

GET THE WOMEN OFF THE WING OR THERE
WILL BE TROUBLE!!!

We were back censoring the mail.

That night we made our way through darkening streets, down to the docks where a rather seedy

B&B had been reserved for us. This would be the uncomfortable haven we would retreat to each night until the dispute was over.

There was another memorable event during our time at Gloucester. I woke up one morning and turned the TV on, to be greeted by a worried looking BBC Announcer describing an explosion at a nuclear power plant in a little town in the Ukraine.

"Great", I thought. "The world's coming to an end and I'm going to die in Gloucester prison."

Chapter 5: The Battles of Lewes

HMP Brockhill, Worcestershire, 2003

We attend our local church after one woman dies at Easter. Rob holds my hand throughout the service. As we exit into the sunlight afterwards the priest is waiting. He knows what has happened and asks how I am. I have held it together but my eyes annoyingly begin to fill. I mumble something about the hope of Easter Day but I don't believe what I am saying. I can't see any empty tomb. Only Golgotha.

Rob tightens his grip on my hand as we walk back to the car.

HMP Lewes, Sussex, 1984 - 1988

My first posting as an Assistant Governor was to HMP Lewes. I was still nipping back to Wakefield for odd weeks as part of the ongoing training. It was Autumn 1984 and I was 22 years old. I had decided, by this stage, that I should ask not to be sent too far away from my aging parents who lived in Brighton. In retrospect this was a bad decision. I ended up spending all my time at Lewes dreading that my mother might catch the bus and turn up at the prison looking for me.

I was allocated a staff quarter a couple of miles away from the prison. It had not been lived in for ages and to my delight, the Works Department agreed to paint it all kinds of lurid colours under my direction. I had a home, now all I needed was company. I visited Raystede Animal Rescue Centre in Lewes and adopted the biggest cat I could spot, hoping he would tough it out against the two beautiful but belligerent looking Siamese cats I had discovered were living next door. My plan wasn't to be entirely successful. He was bullied unmercifully until the day he could stand it no more, when he suddenly leapt off the window sill onto the heads of his grinning persecutors. There were tufts of white fur all over the front garden, until the wind blew them away.

Lewes prison is a small Victorian gaol in the picturesque conservative town of the same name.

The imposing flint gatehouse dominates the main road into the town. Lewes then held male adult prisoners of all categories together with a small number of young men.

The Governing Governor looked a lot like Yuri Andropov. What's more, the first thing he began talking about in his sinister deep voice when he met me on my first morning, was his son who it turned out had been at the same sixth form college as me. That would have been fine, except that he then went on to remark that he had seen me in a play there once. The play referred to had been Cabaret, and my character was a stereotypical prostitute complete with split skirt, plunging neckline and red feather boa. He stared at me with a odd look that I didn't understand. This was rather disconcerting.

Fortunately I didn't need to have much to do with the Governor. My supervisor was the acting Deputy Governor. He resembled Lesley Crowther of Crackerjack fame and was a lovely man with endless patience. Unfortunately for my Lesley-

Lookalike, after a few months he was ousted from his acting Deputy position and it was given to an ambitious Assistant Governor, a young, big, bullish man, who was apparently, "going places". Lesley was furious in his understated way and I was on his side. I disliked the Upstart intensely too, finding him arrogant and patronising. He also brutally rubbished a new fire alarm contingency plan I worked hard on. It may have been a little naive but I just did not think we should kill the prisoners.

An Assistant Governor I was particularly fond of was a sweet little man who looked rather like a bushbaby. One morning an Officer rushed into the Centre office where we were idly chewing the fat, to inform us of a suspicious parcel in the mail room that was ticking. For once in my career, someone actually decided to consult the relevant contingency plan. It read:

'In the event of a suspicious device being discovered, the Duty Governor will carry the item

out of the prison and place it down the drain outside the gate'

We looked at each other. Then all of us agreed that it was the stupidest contingency plan ever written and none of us were doing it. All of us, that is, except the Bushbaby: "Don't worry," declared he, drawing himself up to his full and cuddly 5' 4". "I will carry the bomb".

In admiration (and from a considerable distance) we watched him march off to the gate. Several hours later the 'bomb' turned out to be a cassette recorder that a prisoner's girlfriend had sent in, batteries included, ticking because it had switched itself on.

These were the last days of the Chief Officers, and there were two at Lewes. The younger was a handsome and pleasant man who seemed to do very little, but despite this was well liked by everyone. To be fair, he probably couldn't really do much, as his senior was very much 'in charge'.

The No. 1 Chief was well respected but looked permanently tired. He probably didn't think much of any Governor who had not worked their way up through the ranks, and as the first female governor grade at Lewes, I thought my presence particularly disturbed him.

Initially I was based on the remand wing sharing an office with Lesley. My desk faced the door and I would look out through the door's glass panel onto the ground floor landing. One day I saw the Chief approach but couldn't work out what he was doing. He was performing a strange dipping walk - like some kind of bird mating ritual. Later, after I returned to work after a few days off, I discovered that he had organised a plank of wood to be nailed to the lower half of my desk. He had worked out that if he crouched low enough, he could see my legs through the door. This was clearly a security risk.

I felt for him, though. He was retiring after a lifetime in the Prison Service and things were changing fast. He was really good at his job and yet the powers that be had decided his role, and that of his colleagues, was no longer necessary.

It is interesting that so many Prison Officers still mourn the passing of the Chief Officer, even though most will never have been in the Service during their time. This was the head of the uniformed staff and the person Officers aspired to be. Most then and now don't identify with ex-university students coming in to lead them and few Officers sadly, even now, are promoted right up through the ranks to governor level.

Perhaps to make up for the perceived loss of the Chief Officer and to try to make Governors appear more militaristic for political reasons, right leaning politicians have sometimes attempted to put Governors into uniform. But all plans have been abandoned due to the cost. Actually at times I felt it would have been useful to stand in uniform alongside staff when asking them to put themselves at risk, or sharing their grief at the loss of a colleague. But there is a counter argument. It can be helpful for a prisoner when convinced that the 'system' is against them, to feel that they can speak to someone in authority who isn't in a uniform: it can diffuse the tension.

My supervised period working on the remand wing was extremely frustrating. Lesley would hardly let me do anything by myself, he was so protective. I did have some routine tasks: I took prisoners' 'applications' (requests), such as for an extra visit from family or friends, or to be allowed to spend an additional amount of their private cash in the prisoners' shop than was normally allowed. I checked sentence calculations and interviewed new arrivals. I verified details such as the prisoner's next of kin and their home address. I asked whether they had ever tried to take their own life. One man told me that he had thrown himself down in front of a car but it had stopped. Next he had taken an overdose but woken up. Then he had hung himself from a tree but the branch had broken. He had fallen to the ground and another branch had hit him on the head. "After that", he said, "I thought I was meant to give it a go".

After my supervisory period was up on the remand wing I was paired with Mr Manners, an experienced Principal Officer on the Sentenced Adult and Young Offender wing. On the Assistant Governors' course one of our number had role-played the first meeting between an old PO and a new AG. He had portrayed a cynical character with a grim expression, hauling himself out of his chair when faced by the young and apparently idiotic AG foisted upon him, waving his finger aggressively in the AG's face and barking at him: "Listen while I tell you what you need to know!" Our first meeting was exactly like that. I grew very fond of PO Manners. We shared the same office and got on like a prison on fire. He taught me basic 'gaol-craft' and we made plans together about how to improve the wing. Three years later he was a guest at my wedding.

That wing was a good example of the risks of mixing different types of prisoners.

At the time sentenced young offenders were located on the top landing and adults on the lower landings. The noise, frequent fighting and constant disruption caused by the youngsters sometimes grew too much for their more mature neighbours. One lunchtime right before my eyes, a bunch of adults stormed up the staircases and a mass fight broke out. It was one of the few times I have actually had to hit an alarm bell.

I don't remember much else about my time on that wing except one morning when walking across the exercise yard I heard some bright spark of a prisoner yell down from his cell window high above me: "Your hair needs washing!"

"Damn", I remember thinking, "I thought I could get away with it another day." Sometimes they knew how to get under your skin.

Then I was put in charge of the Lifers Wing.

For the first time I had my own office, it was big and I loved it. I had it painted Wedgwood blue. Afterwards, whenever I had the chance to have my office painted I found myself painting it this same shade. I think it reminded me of the seaside. I made the Works department put up a gigantic board on the wall opposite me with the details of every prisoner I was responsible for and all his review dates. I was very accessible to inmates located where I was, but they would rarely barge in without knocking.

Lewes was a Category B prison which meant that the prisoners were: "*Those who pose a risk to the public but may not require maximum security, but for whom escape still needs to be made very difficult*".

I became fascinated by the men. They were all different. Sometimes I genuinely felt: *"There but for the grace of God go I!"*. There was one quiet older resident Stanley who after a minor altercation with his mate in a pub had given him a slight shove on the way out. His mate had tripped down a step, hit his head and died. Stanley had been given a life sentence for manslaughter. He accepted his situation and had little expectation of being released. He didn't protest. He wasn't one to complain.

Others worried me a lot more. Samuels had been given a life sentence for sexual assaults on women. He had a severe facial deformity and when I joined Lewes he was part-way through a number of major surgeries to correct the disfigurement. Others had tortured and mocked him all his life for looking different and it was believed by his psychiatrists that if this correction could be done, it would reduce his anger and his risk. By the end of my time at Lewes neither I nor my fellow governors had any confidence that this was the case. Samuels, we felt, remained a major risk to women. I don't know what became of him.

One of the most dangerous men on the wing, I was convinced, was Craxley. Already in his late 40s he had only committed one offence in his life. He had stalked a woman for months, followed her home after she had got off the bus, managed to get in her house, and stabbed her to death. Shortly after I took up residence on the Lifer wing Craxley knocked politely on my office door and asked if he could have a word. I nodded. He sat down sedately facing me. He had black hair and bony features and wore glasses like my father had worn in the 1950s. A slight smile was on his face.

"I know where you were today", he said softly.

"Oh yes?" I replied.

He recited with quiet pleasure several places I had been around the town in my lunch break. No doubt he had overheard a member of staff unwisely gossiping. I found this 'surveillance' eerily reminiscent of his crime.

Years later I was to come across Craxley in another prison. He gave me a slow smile; I could tell he recognised me. Intrigued, I later re-read the report I'd written on him in Lewes and examined his consequent prison career. It is often very hard for prisoners to demonstrate that their 'risk' to the public has reduced in prison, particularly if they are not exposed to similar situations and they have no obvious 'issues' such as addiction, to get a grip of. Craxley had behaved impeccably throughout his time but little things that he did at each stage had given cause for concern and his progression had been slow. When I caught up with him, he had just been recalled from an open prison, the final test before being released on licence. In the admin corridor of the gaol, which Craxley had access to, mysterious holes had been found drilled in the walls of the Ladies toilets.

Two years into my time at Lewes Andropov retired and a new Governor arrived, no less a person than John Marriott. This was the same John Marriott who would later be informed that he would no longer be allowed to govern any prison following the escape of three prisoners from Parkhurst. Jeremy Paxman would ask Home Secretary Michael Howard twelve times on Newsnight if he had been responsible for that decision.

John was young, charismatic and a reformer; a breath of fresh air and a rising star. He was very compassionate. The Herald of Free Enterprise ferry sank during his time at Lewes and he did all he could to support a prisoner who had lost family on board.

The country was in the grip of the AIDs terror. A positive diagnosis of HIV or AIDS meant a death sentence and the Prison Service was only just beginning to think about how to handle the crisis. Before any principles had even been thrashed out however, the terror came knocking at the gates of Lewes.

There was a sombre mood in John's office when I walked in. He was sat at his desk, his usual cheerful face for once sober.

"What's happened?" I asked. He didn't look up.

"It's Hoskins". He said. "He's tested positive."

Hoskins was a big pleasant prisoner in his 40s whose job was serving food from the wing hotplate. John and the Doctor went to break the news to him together. I saw Hoskins walk into the office where they were waiting for him. His sleeves were rolled up ready for a day's work. They sat with him for a long time.

As sometimes happens to those who give much and always tend to think the best of people, John was occasionally taken advantage of. A notorious prisoner arrived who had allegedly been involved but not charged with, assisting a prisoner to escape from another prison. He was asking for temporary release.

"Now", said John, "I'm putting my job on the line by letting you out, Jim". He looked the prisoner solemnly in the eyes. "But I trust you."

Did he come back? Did he hell.

I had my own difficult times. One awful evening when I was Duty Governor, a prisoner's relative rang from America wanting to break the news personally to him that his wife had given birth but their newborn twin babies had died. The man was currently in the segregation unit. He was large, muscular. and he was known to be violent when frustrated. I argued that he needed to be told, the relative should do it and it was his right to know as soon as possible. The staff disagreed, wanting to leave it until the morning when more staff would be on duty and any response from the prisoner could be better managed. Blackly and reluctantly, they acquiesced. Four Officers, myself and the prisoner stood around in the wing office while he took the short call. He overturned the table then stormed back to his cell. I had done nothing to build my credibility with these staff. But I still think I was right to allow the call.

I was the first female Assistant Governor at Lewes and my gender and youth was sometimes an issue. I was certainly a novelty. The only other 'operational'[8] woman was an Officer Support Grade who was confined in those days to working in the Gate. There were still no women Prison Officers working in male prisons. I had to endure my share of remarks about women who should be

---

8 The term 'operational' includes: Prison Officers, Governor Grades and Operational Support Grades.

at home pregnant and/or in the kitchen. I also found it grating, if I wasn't full of the joys of spring, that I would immediately be asked what was wrong with me and why I wasn't smiling, by some staff who seemed convinced that I was primarily there to brighten up the place, like a decorative lamp.

One or two staff members however, definitely thought I was a waste of space.

One morning I received intelligence that there was going to be an escape attempt that very afternoon. The plan was ingenious. Over the previous few weeks, a group of prisoners who worked in the kitchen had been hollowing out the insides of a pile of large red plastic milk crates, which had been left carelessly lying around the loading area. Today those crates would be leaving on the milk lorry, with the prisoners concealed inside.

When I rang the Principal Officer in charge of Security he curtly informed me that he was far too busy to talk to me. This man was not my greatest fan. I took a breath. "I'm very sorry to interrupt you but I thought you might *possibly* be interested in knowing about an escape that's going to happen this afternoon, unless we stop it? Do you have a moment to hear me now?"

There was a pleasing dead silence.

As time went on I grew more confident, feeling more free to be myself. I didn't care if they thought I was a bit strange.

An Officer showed me an ancient shoe he had found complete with an incumbent nest of mice. On hearing that he proposed to chuck it in the boiler, I snatched it off him and drove to Stanmer Park in my lunch break to rehome them.

I developed a soft spot though, for many of the staff. Sometimes they cracked me up.
Two Officers were killing time waiting for the roll to be called.

"Tell her your claim to fame, Fred", one said. His mate put his head on one side and half-grinned sheepishly.

"Taken hostage wasn't I!" He said. I began commiserating at how awful that must have been.

His mate interrupted gleefully: "They started off by demanding a helicopter. By the end of it they negotiated him back for a packet of tea bags." He raised his voice. "This man's life is worth a packet of tea bags!" He left the office guffawing with laughter, Tetley Tea's poster boy following cheerfully in his wake.

Most of the staff under a tough exterior could be very gentle.

I was curious about what was happening in the gate. I could see shoe boxes lined up along the counter.

Mice weren't the only wildlife the prison had to deal with. Pigeons were a major problem. Food was put down to dope them after which a prisoner would despatch them. I was to spend some time attempting to convince the Works Department that employing a person already convicted of murder to do the latter was not a good idea, even if he did have relevant experience. Why were there shoe boxes in the gate? The gate staff were nursing all the other wild birds who had also eaten the dope, while they slept off their unexpected naps. I watched an Officer patiently stroking a sparrow to bring it back to life after it had already stopped breathing three times.

It is probably a major character flaw that I have a low threshold for boredom. I soon realised that my favourite part of the job was dealing with incidents (as long as no one ended up getting hurt). At Lewes there were copious amounts of them.

Lewes was a Victorian gaol in a market town with limited ability to improve its perimeter security and this tempted prisoners to chance making bids for freedom. These came in many forms. One day came the rumour that a gun had been manufactured on the Lifer wing. The staff began searching. Half an hour later a brightly coloured cardboard 'tommy-gun' was discovered in the cell of a harmless prisoner named Peterson who had learning difficulties. A wise Senior Officer didn't end the search. A few cells further down the landing staff discovered an extremely realistic black handgun.

Peterson, incidentally, wasn't put off for long by the confiscation of his weapon. A few weeks later a gentleman who owned a house adjacent to the wall, knocked on the prison gate and very politely asked if the prisoner who had made the bow could please stop firing his arrows into their garden as one had only narrowly missed his wife.

The escape attempts were imaginative. One man managed to hide in a laundry van only to find himself up the road in Northeye Prison where the next load was due to be collected. On another occasion, a man escaped in a dustbin lorry. He was recaptured the worst for wear. It turned out he wasn't the only life form hiding there and he was returned to the prison covered head to toe in wasp stings. Bin bags had provided poor protection.

One of the most potentially dangerous escapes was thwarted because of a ripped bed sheet.

First thing every morning, an Officer Support Grade had to patrol the outside of the prison to check the perimeter was secure. This morning, he casually strolled into the Centre Office and remarked that there was a ladder propped up against the wall. Shortly afterwards came the discovery of a bag of tools lying in a gully under one of the wings. A torn strip of sheet tied to a toothbrush was attached to the handle.

After a little head-scratching, we hypothesised that someone had broken into the prison bringing a bag of tools with him: a prisoner had let down the strip of sheet from his window (weighted with a toothbrush), the intruder had tied the sheet to the toolbag to be hauled up and then hastily left the prison the same way he had got in. Unfortunately for the prisoner however, the sheet had ripped, flinging the tools back into the gully.

The bag lay beneath the windows of three cells. One cell contained a known IRA sympathiser. This was 1985 and the year before the IRA had blown up the Grand Brighton Hotel hosting the

Conservative Party conference. The following week the conference was due again - this time in Blackpool. We thought it just possible that this prisoner was being sprung because the IRA wanted him out, with a particular purpose in mind. We kept all three prisoners in the segregation unit for a fortnight pending investigation, and until the conference was over.

One problem I began to struggle with at Lewes was how to handle staff social events. I was part of the leadership team now and felt I ought to attend, but I didn't relish turning up to them on my own. All the other Governors were married and I had no desire to beg anyone to take me along as extra baggage. My personal life was still non-existent. I felt lonely at times (despite the cat), weathered this as best I could by joining a couple of local societies, but this I needed to solve. Feeling extremely nervous and very daring, I took out a subscription for Dateline, the stone-age equivalent of online dating.

After a few hiccups (I met up with one man in a lay-by only to lose him on the bypass) my mission to acquire the necessary beaux was successful and having one of these poor souls in tow I would feel confident enough to attend the events. One evening a young Prison Officer, emboldened by alcohol, asked me to dance. As we circled the room, he with his head resting comfortably on my shoulder, his mates chuckling in the background, I thought: "You're going to regret this tomorrow". I was right. He had asked the Guv'nor to slow dance and the staff weren't going to let him forget it. He couldn't look me in the eye for a month.

I wouldn't let my new Gentlemen Callers stick around for long though. Not even Ryan, a potentially valuable acquisition who had the impressive job of Diamond Driller. He escorted me to Wimbledon Lawn Tennis Club in his convertible and plied me with strawberries and champagne in the stands of Court No 1. He was a nice guy, but I didn't like him enough, unfortunately.

One morning however, a letter fell through my postbox from another prospective suitor. The letter was full of theology and shift patterns. He was a BBC engineer. My first date with Rob was in Al Forno's Pizza restaurant in Brighton. I identified him across the road hopping awkwardly from one foot to another, bearing an enormous bunch of spring flowers. I was glad I had a plastic carrier bag in my handbag to stash them in for the rest of the evening. Rob had very black hair and an impressive moustache, resembling Trevor Eve in his *'Shoestring'* days. There was a gawky sweetness about him. After the meal we walked to the pier and I spent a silly amount of time on the tuppenny falls for which I admitted an addiction. On our second date he turned up in his van an hour early. Arriving home from work I spotted him parked up the road attempting to hide in the footwell. He nearly jumped out of his skin when I banged loudly on the window. For our third date we went on a day trip to France and I flung hot chocolate over both of us. We were clearly meant to be.

Rob introduced me to some of his interesting friends and talked a lot about his passions - chiefly Patrick McGoohan's 'The Prisoner' (irony), Eastern religions, and of course the BBC. I thought Rob should learn something about my odd career too. I dragged him to a staff open evening at the prison where, with some delight, I pointed out that the ham sandwich he'd just eaten had been prepared by a lifer who had kept the head of his victim in his fridge.

But as is usual for those attempting to manage full time jobs and relationships, life began to get tricky. Rob was working long hours, often nights, and on the opposite weekend to me. We barely saw each other and he was shattered when we did. I asked John if I could change weekends; another one of the AGs had said they were willing to swap. John refused but wouldn't give me any reason why. He was also unusually irritated.

Then a bombshell. I arrived one morning to be told John had been 'ghosted'[9]. The charismatic Governor had a secret. Unknown to me, he had been having a relationship with a member of his staff, which was strictly forbidden for Governors, and it had come to the notice of Prison Service HQ. The No. 1 Chief pulled me aside. "I've known he was having an affair for weeks," he said, "I thought it was you". I had thought the Chief had been giving me stranger looks than normal, but had just assumed it was my usual overactive imagination.

A year after we met, Rob and I were married at St Michaels and All Angels church in Lewes. My father-in-law, himself a Rural Dean, officiated together with three other priests.

"This should make it stick," he assured us.

My three bridesmaids were Rob's sister, together with my best friends from university and childhood. Rob brought to the party an eclectic collection of

---

9 Prison slang for being transferred out without warning.

mates who acted their part with enthusiasm as best man, ushers and camera men.

My dad rang me the morning of the wedding to tell me my mother had reported feeling "too tired" and was not coming. She would often have unspecified ailments which would necessitate her retreating to her bed for the day. We had spent a good morning together a few weeks before, when she had chosen a new dress and a hat. They were green and white and she looked pretty in them. In some ways it was a relief she wasn't coming but another side of me felt a stab of loss. And a flash of anger. Dad seemed a lonely figure when he arrived and vulnerable. He quietly and with dignity performed his role.

Other things luckily went according to plan. The horses I'd insisted on having did make it up the hill. Our four year old page boy, Rob's younger brother, didn't fall out of the carriage despite his best efforts. And the Prison Officers, holding their batons over us as we left the church, put up patiently with being repeatedly tweaked by the annoying photographer and resisted the urge to clobber him. It was a great day but when Rob and I drove away after the reception I was glad to leave the crowd behind. But it was hard saying goodbye to my dad.

When we arrived at our hotel we discovered that not only had the bridesmaids and best men found out our location and were threatening to show up, but also that they had filled my suitcase with an inflated helium balloon, a mass of confetti, a furry toy beaver puppet, a wellington boot and a large bottle of horse liniment (no one I know has a horse). We spent some hours the next morning posting it all back. Then we flew to Miami with Virgin Atlantic to enjoy a short cruise and a trip to Disneyland. Very 1985.

Early on we realised that a married life where I continued to work in Lewes while Rob commuted to work for the BBC in London was not sustainable. I had served the usual four years furlough for a Governor at that time and could apply for a transfer. As almost no one in the history of the Prison Service ever asked to move to a London prison voluntarily, my application to do so was almost instantly approved.

Chapter 6: The Scrubs

Civil Service Appeal Board, London, 2003

The atmosphere in the bare white room is tense. The exChair of Brockhill Prison Officers' Association sitting opposite me looks defiant. Her representative whispers in her ear.

The door opens. The judgement is in. The Chair of the Civil Service Appeal Board enters the room, sits down, shuffles his papers and makes his pronouncement: "We uphold the findings of the disciplinary hearing but we find the award too harsh. The appellant should not have been dismissed".

I don't hear any more. My brain is spinning. What the hell do I do now?

HMP Wormwood Scrubs, London, 1988-1992

I was transferred to Wormwood Scrubs in the Autumn of 1988. I was 26. Scrubs was a Victorian titan of a prison holding well over a thousand men of all categories. History hit you in the face when you entered, from the imposing gate with its plaster figures of prison reformers Elizabeth Fry and John Howard, to the monstrous chapel the Governor would play badminton in, upsetting the Chaplain. Four towering parallel wings dominated the site: at their ends gigantic cathedral-like windows glaring down at you accusingly.

This was another place full of animal life: this time feral cats. Dirty and frayed around the edges, hardened by many battles, generations had stalked the yards. I once saw a prison patrol dog, whimpering loudly, drag its handler in the opposite direction when it saw one coming.

Scrubs too had seen its share of infamous residents from Peter Sutcliffe and Ian Brady to the likes of Keith Richards and Lesley Grantham. Shortly after my arrival a member of staff cleared out a wing office and discovered a cardboard box containing the property notorious spy George Blake had failed to take with him, when he had decided the place had lost its charm.

Staff liked to feel Scrubs was a different sort of prison. They took pride in where they worked and looked down on neighbouring gaols like Wandsworth and Pentonville as being rather 'stuck in the mud' and reactionary. They felt Scrubs was much more forward looking, but that wasn't quite the case. In 1979 there had been a major rooftop protest by IRA prisoners over changes to visiting entitlements and since then there had been a series of further serious incidents. Many prisoners and staff had been injured and this wasn't forgotten. Memories are long in the Service. The Prison Officers Association, a dominant force in the gaol, was ready to protect its members from any new perceived threat. When I arrived there, management at Scrubs was in an ongoing struggle to persuade its local Prison Officers Association to co-operate in allowing the prisoners a little more association with their peers. And management didn't seem to be getting anywhere.

Few people talk openly about the genuine fear that prison staff have of prisoners. It is not an unreasonable anxiety but managing risk is not a black and white exercise. The Prison Officers Association was often intransigent and very powerful in many prisons in those days and would oppose most attempts to liberalise the regime for prisoners or work with management to make somewhere more cost-effective. It was to take the brutal threat and then partial imposition of privatisation, with some dire consequences for both staff and prisoners, to diminish some of that power.

On arrival Rob and I were lucky enough to be allocated one of the last Governor's quarters at Scrubs - a mock Tudor effort in West Acton. It was convenient both for the prison and the BBC. We were incredibly fortunate to live somewhere so pleasant. It was a lovely house and conveniently near the Tube. We found only one slight disadvantage. Our cat proved to have separation issues and developed a sneaky habit of attempting to follow us to work. At the ticket office he would start panicking and loudly announce his presence and would then have to be picked up, marched home and flung through the front door in the hope that we could hotfoot it back to the Tube before he made it out again through the cat flap.

I arrived for my first day at Scrubs to find I was again deployed to work with Lifers - on 'D' Wing.

My desk and chair faced the door and dwarfed the prison cell which comprised my office. High in the wall above my head was a tiny barred window which didn't let in much natural light. On the wall was a large poster of the unknown man holding back the tank in Tiananmen Square. Maybe this iconic image had helped to fortify a previous inhabitant of the office. I left it up.

On the wing I was one of three Governor '5's (the new name for Assistant Governors). In charge of us was a Governor '4'. We worked alongside a Principal Officer, Senior Officers, Prison Officers, three Probation Officers and a team of psychologists.

The Principal Officer who effectively ran the wing was a huge bear of a man, slow of speech and shrewd: he had seen it all, including the last riot. His claim to fame was that he would hardly ever stand up. If he was roused enough to haul himself to his feet you knew something serious was happening. This technique, or simple lack of desire to exert himself, helped do its bit, I always thought, to calm the place. Several years later I re-visited Scrubs and to my distress found the Bear terribly changed, he had been seriously ill and was a shadow of his former self.

There were so many senior and specialist staff working on D wing, partly for historical reasons (we were shortly to be culled), but mainly because of the high volume of report writing required. This was because we received newly sentenced lifers straight from the courts. We spent days assessing them and writing reports in order to try to decide the levels of security a man needed and the most appropriate prison to send him to next.

Apart from report writing one of my routine duties was allocating prisoners to work. I was informed by Rob that my personality became quite warped by this responsibility. The News would broadcast details about some grisly murder and show photos of the villain who had been given his just desserts, and more than once I would be heard to murmur: "Good...young...looks fit...should be able to wear industrial safety boots...". Finding enough men able to work in the aluminium window shop was the bane of my life.

I also had to hear prisoners' complaints. The Governors' offices were right at the end of the wing. A disgruntled prisoner would air his grievance first with wing staff, move onto the Senior Officers, then visit the Bear (who would not stand up). If he remained unsatisfied, he would bang loudly on each of the Governors' offices working his way down the wing. If you were unluckily enough to be in the last occupied office that day, the buck stopped with you.

One afternoon I was in situ and a prisoner didn't like what I said. He stormed out and put his very large fist straight through the reinforced glass panel of the office opposite. I was grateful to him for choosing that and not my face.

Usually the grievances were about food. Prison caterers are only given a pittance to spend on each prisoner, and most of the time the results weren't too awful. But sometimes I did feel that they were taking the mickey. I discovered early on a strategy that worked: I just had to consume some of whatever was proffered by complaining prisoners and pretend it was at least palatable. It was a good thing I had a strong stomach. One lunchtime a prisoner presented me with a thin yellow skin of what optimistically had been described as 'rice pudding'. "My God!" I heard him say as he left the office, "she ate it!"

I settled in quickly but as a young woman, particularly one that did not wear a uniform, I still sometimes had to prove my credibility.

A short time after my arrival, late in the morning when I was finishing writing up a report in the wing board room, a prisoner knocked on the door and asked to speak to me. Glancing nervously over his shoulder, he informed me that he knew another man was going to be seriously assaulted that afternoon. Outside I could hear the usual wing noises. It was nearing the time for the prison roll to be counted; staff began shouting for prisoners to 'bang up' and doors started slamming. A couple of minutes later, having extracted the necessary information, I sent the prisoner on his way.

Straight afterwards Mr Smart, a young Officer with a couple of years' experience, who clearly thought he knew it all, barged into the room and attempted to tell me off in a very patronising manner, for talking to prisoners outside of the time slot in which I was 'supposed' to see them. Ticked off, I rose to my feet and became my most direct, explaining in no uncertain terms and in some detail, exactly why it had been necessary for me to hear the prisoner out.

I discovered afterwards, another member of staff had overheard the conversation, as the boardroom walls were very flimsy, and soon an account of my 'bollocking' (usual prison terminology) of the Officer was common knowledge. It seemed to do my credibility no harm at all.

Lifers continued to fascinate me. Some men would move on quickly to other prisons after assessment. Others would settle in for the long term and they made an effort to make their cells homely. Many would purchase rugs and bedspreads and attach photos of loved ones to the walls. (A hot tip for DIY-ers: toothpaste works nearly as well as blutack but does leave permanent marks on the wall.) 'Model' (well behaved) prisoners were allowed to keep caged birds and men would become very close to these tiny creatures. Sometimes you could hear them singing. It probably sounds strange and romantic to imagine prisoners with birds in their cells nowadays, but back then it was commonplace. Signs would appear on cell doors:

KNOCK BEFORE ENTERING
BUDGIE LOOSE

Many men were complete unknown quantities. Some were Category A prisoners: *'those that would pose the most threat to the public, the police or national security should they escape'*. A few were very dangerous indeed.

One man genuinely spooked me. He had murdered three women who had been employed as sex workers. As he sat in my cramped office I could feel the hairs on the back of my neck rising, finding myself mentally calculating if I would be able to hurl myself across my desk to the alarm bell, before he got to me. A woman Probation Officer told me afterwards she had had the same visceral reaction.

I had few uncomfortable interactions, but there was one instance which really disturbed me. I read in a report the words a victim, an elderly lady, had whispered to her murderer as she had pleaded with him not to kill her. The prisoner had not been able to forget them, and neither will I.

Some men knew how to play the system. Prisoners would be paid a few pounds for working and would spend the money on sweets or cigarettes or toiletries. The best job on the wing was 'Staff Tea Boy' and it did not come up very often. I watched a quiet but determined prisoner, Overton, set out to get the job. He was a bespectacled middle aged man who had recently killed his wife, and he gave everyone the impression that he would not have a clue how to survive in prison. Appearances were deceptive. He was always somewhere in the background, ready to carry a tray or generally assist when the official incumbent might need it. Like the slimey Chameleon from Monsters Inc. he learnt just the right amount of obsequiousness without being too annoying. It worked. When the job came up he was the natural choice, and to be fair he made a good cup of tea.

There was a well established hierarchy in the prison. At the bottom were those known to have hurt children. They could try lying about why they were in prison but eventually their crimes would be discovered and then their days were numbered. They would be rapidly escorted off the wing to be segregated - probably for the rest of their sentence. Slightly higher up the tree were those who had committed offences against women. However, sexism being endemic, allowances were sometimes made for those whose victims were deemed to have been 'asking for it'. At the top of the tree were those convicted of serious gangland crimes.

Although D wing was full of new lifers, occasionally existing prisoners from other places would pass through. One morning the atmosphere was different: a celebrity was in their midst and the men were in awe. It was Reggie Kray, one half of the notorious Kray twins who had run one of the biggest gangs in the East End of London during the 1950s and 60s. Murders, protection rackets and armed robberies were all in a day's work for them. They caused terror to many and were lionized by others. Reggie was a hero to most of the criminals in our care. He called by my office: "Good morning, Mrs Treen," he said. He had found out my name. "I had hoped to stay here for a while". He added graciously: "I'm sorry I won't get to work with you".

The men came to judgement on their peers quickly. There was a ruckus on the wing. Prisoner Cumings was being removed to the segregation unit for his own protection, accompanied by a chorus of furious shouts and bangs.

"What happened?" I asked the Senior Officer.

"Cumings lost it over something", he replied. "Then he attacked his budgie".

The Governors attempting to run the place were very different characters.

The Governing Governor was a clever man but slippery as an eel. He had a strange talent: no one really understood what he said, but no one dared to tell him. He talked in a weird gobbledygook way which gave you the gist, but it wasn't possible to follow the actual words. It made people who didn't know him feel that he was very wise, and they were a bit stupid.

The Eel's gut judgement about the prison was pretty good and we respected that, however he was often absent and didn't do a lot of actual work (as we working grades defined it) while he was there. I later discovered a drawer stuffed full of two years' worth of annual staff reports he should have written, which would tend to confirm this judgement.

The Eccentric was a man with a brilliant mind. A Governor '4', he ambled cheerfully around the prison, resembling an extra-dishevelled Patrick Moore. He wore a green waxed jacket he never took off summer or winter and may indeed have slept in. Sometimes he was forced to go on training courses but he didn't take a bag, he just stuffed everything into the many pockets of that jacket. He was happily married to 'She who Must be Obeyed,' who he pretended to be frightened of and talked about all the time. He held court in the prison mess every lunchtime telling stories to entertain us all.

As a report writer he wasn't much good. The only thing I ever saw him write, when cornered, was a brief memo scrawled on a napkin. But as an adjudicator he was marvellous. One day the tension in the prison was palpable. A popular prisoner had been restrained in full view of his peers after allegedly assaulting an Officer. He had been taken to the segregation unit, all the time screaming that he had been beaten up by staff. Memories of the recent riot were in everyone's minds and people were nervous. In the seg the excited prisoner was now demanding half the wing be called as witnesses at his forthcoming adjudication. The Eccentric was to officiate.

"What are you going to do?" we asked him at lunch. He carried on munching.

"Oh I'm going to call everyone. The whole wing if necessary. I'm going to take my time. Go into it VERY thoroughly".

The strategy worked. The adjudication took three weeks. By the end the whole prison was bored stiff of it and the tension had vanished.

Another Governor 4 - Joe - was a would-be thespian like me. We used to attend all his endeavours and join in the cat calling as he played a succession of heroes, nazis and pirates.

In 1989, Joe, I and others were dispatched to Wandsworth during the latest industrial dispute. Most of the staff had walked out and the situation was perilous. The prison was so vast that this time the police were drafted in to help us. The presence of police on the landings wound the men up. Most prisoners retain an intense dislike for the people who catch them, while growing to at least tolerate those whose hands feed them. We, however, saw one practical advantage of the police presence and quickly made good use of the impressive mobile canteen they brought with them, serving an array of hot food at all hours. The Prison Service never rose to anything so generous.

Wandsworth had its lighter moments. We received a high number of applications from prisoners to be allowed to have their heads shaved, which we were granting. The reason was, I found out later, Wandsworth staff didn't allow it as it encouraged the men to look and behave 'hard'. I would like to have been a fly on the wall to hear what the staff said when they returned to find their newly bald population.

It was a very dangerous environment though. A day into the dispute Joe was briefly taken hostage - a truly terrifying experience. I sat next to him on the coach on the way home that night. That was the only time I've ever advised someone to go out with his mates and get drunk. I felt he needed to get talking - fast. Later he left the Service and went to work for a national charity.

There is a postscript to my time at Wandsworth. A few months later a letter appeared in my pigeon hole in Scrubs. It was from a frightened prisoner I had met at Wandsworth. In the letter he called me an *'angel in his darkness'*. I was shocked as I could only have spent a few minutes with him. It revealed to me how desperate some prisoners were for a tiny bit of compassion and attention. And how terrified many are when things get out of hand. There were more than a hundred vulnerable men at Wandsworth, segregated because of their offences or other reasons. If control of the prison had been lost, they would have been completely at the mercy of their ruthless peers.

The youngest governor grades at the Scrubs were the Lads. The Lads were Governor 5s like me. One of these was another of the perpetually youthful and would forever be referred to as the Boy. The other youngster, Gary, was a trifle accident prone. The Lads, Rob and I often used to hang around together outside of work. We were roughly the same age and Rob didn't drink, which was an asset as he used to drive the Lads home in our little black van. One night walking back to the 'Passion Wagon', as it had been christened, Gary mysteriously vanished. After a while he turned up again looking considerably worse for wear. He had leapt over a railing to answer a call of nature, failing to notice that there was a three metre drop on the other side.

On another occasion Gary nearly killed Clarence (the same Governor who was responsible for the tale of Parsley the Lion.)   Gary owned a large white rabbit and when we went round to his house one evening he handed it to Clarence to stroke. It rewarded him with a major asthma attack.

Gary did however manage to sort out one of the most difficult lifers we had to deal with. This was Bates, a young man who could appear truly frightening. The whole of his face, neck and body were covered in tattoos and he would regularly stick his fist in your face, screaming and swearing, while he recited some, usually imagined, grievance.

After the visits period had finished one afternoon, Gary received a complaint from staff that in the large busy visiting room, full of families, Bates and his wife had progressed from enthusiastic fondling to attempted full-on sex. When Bates had been ordered - and ordered again - to stop, he had become abusive. Gary duly wrote to Mrs Bates, advising her that a repeat of this behaviour would result in her being banned from visiting.

Three days later I was in my office on the wing, when I heard a massive crash. I ran out to see Bates rampaging down the landing hunting for Gary. I wasn't the only spectator: staff and prisoners alike had all shot out to see what was happening. We were rewarded by hearing Bates scream: "That wasn't the wife you "C***", it was the wife's sister!"

Slowly the whole wing began to laugh. And laugh. And laugh. Bates was never quite as frightening again.

As usual I lived for the exciting and bizarre incidents that always occur in prisons.

One man escaped from his bed while at the Hammersmith hospital by jumping out of the window, landing on the roof of a car (a Renault Clio I seem to remember). That must have made an interesting insurance claim. He was recaptured quite quickly: he wasn't hard to spot. There are reasons why we take prisoners' clothes away when they are in hospital and force them into 1950s' style pyjamas.

I was duty governor when some dog handlers intercepted a patrol of boy scouts by the wall who, armed with grappling hooks, were attempting to make their own movie. They hadn't planned that final scene.

On another occasion we received a call that a bomb had been placed in the prison. I drove there to find that four Police Officers and a dog had also showed up. We decided that if there was a bomb it would be in the visits complex. I watched somewhat cynically as the dog went through the bins. I suspected he was looking for food as he chewed everything up. I hoped that detecting explosives wasn't what he was trained for. If it was he was heading for a brief career.

Much as I adore dogs, my opinion of specialist dogs was to remain somewhat jaded. Patrol dogs, usually impressive looking Alsatians, are effective at encouraging prisoners to move along when they are expected to, and occasionally will nab a fleeing escapee. Saying that however, I did hear of one in the heat of the moment biting his handler and another two dogs deciding it was a good moment to consummate their relationship. All the drugs dogs I personally saw deployed though, never actually found anything. That's not to say that they had no purpose: when prisoners heard them coming they would flush their stash down the toilet. They had more faith in them than I did. This sums it up: Handler to Governor: "I thought he indicated Ma'am, he rushed into the showers. I could hardly hold him".

"What was it?"

"He was thirsty".

Terrible incidents happened too of course.

After one suicide I was grateful to the Eel for taking over from me at the hospital where I had gone to meet the man's relatives. One of my colleagues had returned ashen-faced on a previous occasion, after a prisoner's wife had attacked him before running away screaming.

A young, very effeminate lifer arrived on D wing. Marshall was confident, very talkative and too loud. We knew he would attract a lot of attention and warned him of the risks. He was raped by a gang of others within a fortnight. I felt ashamed that we had failed to protect him. He should not have had to pretend to be lesser than himself. The police were called in and Marshall gave a statement and submitted to a medical examination. I don't know how he coped afterwards or if anyone was eventually charged: he immediately went into segregation and was transferred out.

The number of prisoners who suffer rape and sexual assault in our prisons is appalling. Few, through terror and shame, report officially what has happened to them. This is a hidden horror in this country and every other around the world, and attracts no public interest. It continues to make me angry that as a society we don't seem to care. People who come to prison do not lose their rights as humans. It's not like people aren't aware. The perennial cheap joke about the folly of bending over to pick up the soap in a prison shower is a sitcom favourite.

After two years on the Lifer wing I was given an office next to the Governor's and made 'Head of Personnel and Training for Operational Staff' - catchy title. Many seemed to get into various degrees of difficulty. The most serious offenders were an Officer who was reported to me for allegedly beating his wife, Senior Officer Leith who was convicted of shoplifting, and an Officer who didn't turn up to work and was eventually discovered that morning in court, attempting to defend himself against historic child sexual offences.

Mr Leith was a very able Senior Officer in his late thirties, popular and the only male 'out' gay uniformed member of staff I ever met. His shop-lifting offence appeared to have been a genuine one-off, in a moment of stress. What was notable to me was the succession of staff who came to me to plead his case, prefacing all their remarks along the lines of : *"I know he's 'you know' but he's really very good at his job and a sound bloke"*.

Staff themselves had their own pecking order of what constituted more acceptable, or less acceptable misdemeanours. They were often sympathetic to someone alleged to have used excessive force on a prisoner. Perhaps they sensed in themselves how they might 'lose it' one day in the face of constant provocation. In contrast, they had no sympathy whatsoever for staff who trafficked with prisoners, bringing in contraband like drugs or mobile phones or doing other favours for money. That took planning and deceit and was premeditated. Those staff, in their eyes, had most definitely 'crossed the line'.

There is sometimes corruption in the Prison Service. Some individuals manage to slip through the recruitment net and join for the wrong reasons. Some exploit vulnerable prisoners for their own ends. A few are seduced by prisoners for money, love or sex against all rhyme and reason, ending up corrupted and 'serving time' themselves. A tiny minority of staff enjoy the power that their position gives them. Wise managers become suspicious if the same Officer volunteers too readily when a prisoner needs to be moved using force. Or the same Officer is assaulted more often than their peers. It might be that they are more courageous, or more likely to enforce rules than another, or it might be for more sinister reasons.

The vast majority of staff however, I knew, did a challenging job very well, for pay significantly below that of a Police Officer, and at some considerable risk to themselves at times.

Moreover their work remained invisible and unappreciated by the public whom they helped to keep safe, and when featured in the press Prison Officers were inevitably portrayed negatively.

In my new role I spent a lot of time listening to staff and occasionally members of their family. I would receive telephone calls saying things like: *"Please don't tell my husband...he's getting really hard to live with...he really needs that transfer"*.

Staff and their families were often in a very difficult situation. Many staff had come from the North of England and taken jobs at Scrubs because these were the only Prison Service posts then available. Families were either left at home, or their partners had come with them only to return, unable to settle. Sometimes they maintained long-distance relationships for years. But more often than not, relationships failed.

I was now responsible for the ongoing training of the operational staff. One of the identified training needs was 'Race Relations' as it was called at the time. The Prison Service faced a major challenge given some deeply entrenched prejudiced attitudes at every level (including senior managers). Institutionalised racism was an unknown concept.

People from black and ethnic minority groups were (and still are) vastly and disproportionately overrepresented within every layer of the Criminal Justice System - including the prisons. In contrast there were hardly any staff from black or ethnic minority groups.

I witnessed my first stark example of how hard someone has to work, if they are a minority, to be seen as an equal. We had a new Officer of Indian origin working at the Scrubs and I was forever being told how much he was struggling. He wasn't, he was perfectly average and reasonably competent: he was just never going to set the world on fire. If he was white no one would have batted an eyelid.

A group of us went off to be taught how to train up others in Race Relations. It's obvious now that these courses were completely inadequate, but it was a start.

Our time away was happy. I can't remember what we were taught but I know we visited several faith communities including a Sikh Gurdwara and met some lovely people. We came back fired up with enthusiasm, although I soon realised, not exactly up-skilled.

I formed a small team and we attempted to deliver Race Relations training. We were an all white group. At that point there were no middle or senior managers from black or ethnic minority groups at Scrubs. Our first efforts to train were not great. A few of the sessions, always those with all white staff, were truly terrible. Those with the new women Officers, to my horror, were the worst. I had naively assumed that women would empathise with others having to fight prejudice. Perhaps they felt they had to appear 'hard' among their new male peers. Groups with older black staff were not much better. These staff tended to laugh along and nod when prejudiced views were uttered. That is no doubt what they had had to do to survive.

Groups that worked best were those that contained our few young black staff. These staff (however they might have felt inside) appeared confident, talking about their own experiences and challenging some of their colleagues' views. The other groups that worked well to my surprise, were groups with Irish staff. They talked freely about what it was like to have grown up experiencing prejudice.

My attempts to train were not a success. I am not a natural teacher and the attitudes of a few of the staff just used to make me bubble up with impotent frustration and anger. I simply didn't have the skills or experience to constructively challenge them. Eventually I sacked myself and left it to others better able.

One easier task I had was to write speeches for the Eel to give when staff retired. One completely foxed me. Mr Edwards was a lovely elderly Officer who had worked at the Scrubs for over 30 years. He was short, inclined to stoutness and always had a smile on his face. I trawled files, interrogated those that knew him but was at a loss to come up with anything interesting to say. He appeared to have no hobbies, had never been involved in any amusing or embarrassing incidents and nothing remarkable had ever happened to him. He just did his job quietly and competently.

This was the one occasion when the Eel's unique skills as an orator reigned supreme. In the Officers' Club I watched as Mr and Mrs Edwards (who were both of similar stature to each other) stood there proudly smiling, holding hands, while the Eel rambled on. No one understood the words but everyone got how much this harmless old man was loved and respected. People cried at the end: it was one of the best retirement events I've been to.

During my third year at the Scrubs I applied for promotion. I didn't get it. I wasn't the only one. The

Eccentric also applied and was refused. Allegedly he had pulled some coins out of that jacket, slammed them down on the desk and bet those interviewing him that overtime would have to be brought back. He was, of course, right, but they had to call it something else.

The next thing to happen to me was far more important than promotion. Rob and I had always hoped to have children and we were over the moon when we discovered in June 1990 that I was pregnant.

Walking around Scrubs obviously 'with child' caused a degree of nervousness among the staff, particularly when I would march onto the Lifer wing during the association period when prisoners were unlocked; but no one stopped me doing my job. Once, out of mischief, heavily pregnant, I held a gate open to see if I could persuade the Chair of the Prison Officers Association to walk through it ahead of me, but he couldn't bring himself to do it.

I chose to give birth at the Hammersmith Hospital, positioned right next to Scrubs, because we could park in the prison car park avoiding the risk of being clamped and I could nip out of work for antenatal scans. One had to be practical.

In 1991 at 3.30am one March morning after seventeen hours of induced labour, Daughter Number One finally put in an appearance. As I was wheeled out of the delivery room staring at the tiny adorable pink bundle nestled by my side I felt humbled that we had been given the privilege of raising her, and vowed that we would do our best.

My parents visited. Sweetly they brought with them my childhood cuddly koala. Unfortunately, my mother had decided to put it through the washing machine beforehand and as a result it resembled roadkill. This struck me as very funny. Apparently I had a worryingly long bout of hormone-induced giggles.

The Pageboy visited, now 8 years old. He had an allergic reaction to London having been raised in the Fens and spent most of the time in A&E.

The Lads thoughtfully came as well. To their horror they found me attempting to breastfeed. "I told you she'd be doing that," One muttered grimly to the other.

Six months later the Lads were to trek all the way into darkest Norfolk to attend our baby's christening. They arrived with armfuls of root vegetables they'd won off locals in a pub en route. They nobly kept the Pageboy amused, playing cricket with him in the garden all that sunny afternoon.

Before the birth, after much agonising, we had finally decided that Rob would take a career break. It made sense. I was earning the higher salary, working part-time wasn't allowed then in either of our jobs, and neither of us wanted to put our baby into full time childcare. Moreover the BBC Rob had loved was rapidly changing. Engineering was being subcontracted to a private company and Rob would either have to leave to work for them or seek a management position at the BBC, which he had no inclination for. The long shifts and nights were also taking their toll on him. Role-reversal parenting was an unusual choice in those days. In the future Rob's fondness for the old BBC and a few nasty remarks from others would occasionally give me a stab of worry for the choice we had made, such is the guilt that society lays on women, but we always knew that it was the right decision for us.

After three months off, I returned to work and Rob took over. I would arrive back home in the evening to de-brief him on the events of the day, and on one memorable occasion to examine the contents of a nappy he had carefully preserved, which he thought were 'worrying'. Then I would take over and do the night feeds. Both of us adapted to the new arrangements with delight and total unmitigated exhaustion.

A few months passed operating this new arrangement but we were already planning our next move. Both of us knew we wanted to raise our baby out of London and having served four years at Scrubs I was able to ask for a transfer. Then the three of us spent two very painful hours stuck in a queue of traffic trying to get into a car park in Ealing Broadway. The attractions of the Big City had definitely faded. It was time to go.

Chapter 7: Not Yet Men

HMP Brockhill, Worcestershire, 2002

In a moment of madness we have signed up for a short adventure holiday on Dartmoor. Daughter Number 2 by now has now proved herself remarkably adept at learning ways to get other people to do what she wants. She screams constantly until the enthusiastic but harassed expedition leader resorts to hauling her up the entire granite rock face rather than making her climb it. Now, while the rest of us are struggling to manufacture a raft out of oil drums and tarpaulins, she is being towed serenely around the lake by him in a little canoe.

Then my phone rings. It is the call I have been dreading.

HMYOI Aylesbury, Buckinghamshire, 1992-1997

I arrived at Her Majesty's Young Offender Institution Aylesbury in early Spring 1992. I was 30 years old. Finally I was older than those I was in charge of and I quite liked the idea of that. Maybe I thought, I might be able to make more of an impact on youngsters, than those so many years older than myself.

We moved to a little village near Bicester, ideally situated in the middle of a cluster of prisons. The hope was that I might manage to work my way round all of them without having to move again. It was a good theory but it didn't quite come off. I never actually worked at the three nearest gaols. Despite this it proved a good decision. There was a horse in the field opposite, a handsome, if vicious, goose lived round the corner, and in the first few days we were there, we spotted hares in the moonlight, in our lane. It was a world away from the London metropolis.

Aylesbury is a medium size prison, built on the outskirts of the town centre. It held around 400 long term young offenders aged 18 to 21. Aylesbury, too, had seen a recent riot. It was another Victorian radial gaol with high galleried wings. At twilight, if you walked through the fields around the back of the prison you could see white streaks glistening across and up the walls like snail trails. Prisoners would be hanging 'lines' out of their cell windows - thin strips of torn sheets attached to contraband such as cannabis or 'burn' (tobacco).

It wasn't the best environment for anyone. At this point prisoners were still 'slopping out'. Cells were equipped with white plastic lidded chamber pots and each morning would see a noisy procession of young men, arms outstretched, enroute to the 'recesses' (toilet area) to empty them. The smell on the wings first thing was appalling. I was fortunate, I usually didn't arrive until after 'slop-out'. Many prisoners, preferring not to spend the night with the contents, would wrap them in newspaper and lob them out of their cell windows. The next day the unlucky members of the unofficially named 'Shit Patrol' would spend several hours touring the prison scooping them up.

Prisoners at Aylesbury had committed some of the worst crimes in the prison system: serious assaults, drug offences and killings. Many were held on Indeterminate Sentences (the equivalent of adult Life Sentences).

It was a different kettle of fish working at Aylesbury due to the nature of these youngsters. As well as being convicted of serious offences they inevitably had backgrounds of abuse, neglect and abandonment. Where they did have family, their siblings or parents were often also residing at 'Her Majesty's Pleasure'. Due to this or other reasons such as family breakdown, many had spent time in the Care system.

What struck me as particularly sad was these boys' isolation. They often said they wanted to join the army. It offered the prospect of a ready-made family and friends, discipline and structure. Unfortunately the convictions of most of them would automatically rule this out.

Most of our prisoners had limited attention spans and even less self-control. They had few social skills and little insight. Fights and assaults were commonplace - over anything at all. Once I berated a prisoner for bullying another. He seemed genuinely confused why smacking his neighbour round the head every morning when they met enroute to the recesses was wrong: "But it's what everyone does, Miss!"

Rob recalls how I came home one evening and reported that one young man had continued to deny that it was he who had assaulted another, until we'd found part of his victim's ear under his pillow. I don't remember that incident now, it would have been pretty much par for the course.

The average literacy age of all prisoners in the system then was 11 years old and at Aylesbury it was probably lower. Many had been excluded from school. In prison, we had the hope, for the first time, some would learn to read and write, or gain another useful skill.

For some though it was definitely an uphill struggle. I sat in on a pre-release course where a Probation Officer was patiently reinforcing to a lad again and again, the importance of not swearing continually, if ever interviewed for his dream job - working in McDonalds. After listening for a while I was not hopeful about his prospects. These seemed to be the only words he knew.

Few were master criminals. One young felon had tried to rob a bank but found it closed having forgotten to check the opening hours. He had then tried to hold up a nearby corner shop but the irate elderly lady who owned it had promptly slammed the till down hard on his fingers. The police caught up with him in A&E.

A prisoner was brought before me for an adjudication charged with stealing and using another inmate''s phone card.

"It's not true, Miss!" he protested, looking injured, "he was speaking to my mate and I just wanted to say hello".

"OK" I said. "What's the name of your mate"?

He paused for a moment..."John Smith".

I summoned the alleged victim back into the room. I asked him the name of the lad that he had been phoning. He looked surprised.

"Mohammed Hassan", he replied. The accused, listening, shrugged his shoulders and grinned, sometimes it was a fair cop.

One of their favourite past-times was attempting to brew 'hooch'. There weren't masses of drugs coming into Aylesbury in those days; we were confident of that as mandatory drugs testing had just been introduced for class B drugs. Instead inmates would steal a banana or an apple from the kitchen, stick it in a tub of water under their bed and hope for the best. They didn't really seem to understand the concept of yeast. Prison 'hooch' could often be lethal but their efforts weren't usually that toxic. They had no idea what they were doing.

Whatever their problems however, you felt that there was some hope of these young people growing up, learning something and reducing their risk to the public. With the young there is always hope. Despite the appalling crimes many had committed, these were not yet men.

Most Prison Officers at Aylesbury were excellent, particularly as they frequently risked getting hurt breaking up fights. I witnessed an Officer in the segregation unit interviewing a prisoner carried down there for the third time in as many days, leaving a trail of bruised staff behind him. "Now remember what we talked about", he was saying patiently to the now subdued figure standing in the middle of the cell, the fight drained out of him, "about taking two steps forward and one step back…"

My own team at Aylesbury was great, I was fond of them all. They were as mischievous and clever as foxes.

One of my Senior Officers, Mac, had long hair, a red convertible and was very cheeky. He reminded me of Private Walker in 'Dad's Army'. He went on to be an entertaining and inimitable trainer at the Prison Service College.

I nicknamed one of my Principal Officers: 'Speedy Gonzales'. I had good reason.

Around 4pm one afternoon we were informed that a prisoner whom we had let out on day release to the town, had failed to return on time. Convinced he'd 'done a runner', Speedy shot down to the railway station and, without hesitation, stopped the London train from departing. The young man was eventually found in McDonald's finishing the remains of a bag of chips, a bemused look on his face, wondering what all the fuss was about.

Speedy was a dear, but he was impetuous. He arrived back from holiday and I asked him if he had enjoyed himself.

"It was fantastic", he replied enthusiastically. As always he spoke fast as if he was in a rush. "Except that the caravan got stuck on a bridge. There was a notice saying it was too narrow, but I thought I'd give it a go".

I was really lucky, the team worked hard and did their best for me. They were to present me with a large chart: it was titled 'The Family'. It was a family tree with all our real and unofficial names on it. I was at the head, with my nickname '*Joan Baez*'. I was flattered: I quite fancied myself as a rebel.

Life was never dull at Aylesbury. That's probably why I enjoyed working there so much.

In those days, before the Tory Government put pay to such things, staff were allowed to take carefully selected young prisoners away camping to gain their Duke of Edinburgh's awards. One evening I received a call from somewhere on Dartmoor informing me that our whole group of prisoners had disappeared. This was a first. Three hours later I received another message. They had been discovered in a pub. I was impressed, they had trekked right across the moor and found the only hostelry for miles. I felt that deserved some kind of badge.

Our young men did occasionally demonstrate their initiative. Then we were allowed to temporarily release a few to attend swimming lessons at a pool in the town centre. A furious market trader arrived, banging on the gate, demanding to speak to the Governor. Somehow, one of our charges had successfully managed, en route to his weekly lessons, to meet, form a relationship with, and impregnate his daughter.

One day did not start well. As I was driving up to the prison I discovered all the approaching roads cordoned off. I leaned out of the car window and spoke to a Police Officer.

"It's the prison", he said, "Suspect device". I pointed out that, embarrassingly, that as the Governor was away, I was actually in charge and it would be helpful if they could let me in. They allowed me to park up and approach with caution.

The tiny control room was over the gate, up a narrow spiral staircase. I made my way up and squeezed into the room, now crowded with all our senior staff. Entering the prison I had, I discovered, walked straight past the device. It had been detected when it was put through the X-ray machine at the gate, carried back outside and placed in the little garden area out front. This wasn't an ideal location for two reasons: firstly, if the device exploded it would take out the gate, the control room and all of us. Secondly, as the Police Inspector who had now arrived pointedly informed us, by placing it adjacent to the public highway, we had necessitated the shutting down of the whole of Aylesbury's main road system.

The X-ray of the package was convincing. It was clearly an electronic device, with batteries and wires attached. The bomb squad had been summoned, but they would be a while. What followed was another valiant *"I will carry the bomb"* moment. Happily I was automatically excused because as Governor-in-Charge I was deemed to be not entirely expendable. The Head of Works leapt forward. The Police Inspector immediately voiced a more professional version of *"On your own head be it!"*. We watched with interest on CCTV as our hero carried the device out of the garden, down the road, all round the wall and right into the middle of the adjacent field. We gave a collective sigh of relief. We continued to watch as, inexplicably, he then returned and about a metre from the package, slowly and meticulously coned it off.

A couple of hours later the bomb squad arrived.

"Apparently it's addressed to you Ma'am." I was informed. It crossed my mind that this might be an assassination attempt on my life.

Nothing so dramatic: it was my pager that had been sent off to be repaired.

In retrospect I don't remember feeling any fear at all at the prospect of potentially being blown up. I just remember being excited. Perhaps I didn't believe what was happening was real. Or perhaps I just liked the excitement.

A few days later one mid-morning when I was in charge, I discovered we had a 'situation'. I walked onto the wing to find a young man running everywhere, up and down the three gallery landings, brandishing a large home-made knife. He was tall, leggy, with wild hair and he was yelling that if he didn't get what he wanted, he was going to stab himself. He was literally holding himself hostage. The staff were trying to reason with him but wisely keeping their distance. We had quite a problem: at that point all the rest of the wing's inhabitants were elsewhere at work or doing other activities, but shortly they needed to return. There was no way we could allow them to walk in on this.

We had to contain the prisoner and disarm him as quickly as possible. I authorised three lots of 'three-man teams' to kit themselves up in full 'Control and Restraint' gear (bodysuits, helmets, long shields) and enter the wing simultaneously via the different landings. It was like a bizarre kind of pac-man as the teams pushed the furious young man round the wing until eventually, he got tired and gave up. No one was hurt, and the rest of the wing ambled back in at the correct time none the wiser. Ironically the Governor, when reporting the incident to HQ afterwards, was told that I should not have done what I did as I hadn't been on the course training me how to do it. At least they stopped short from telling me off for using my initiative.

Prison is often a tense place and the dynamic of managing a diverse population, most of which does not want to be there, is to say the least, tricky. Staff are completely outnumbered by prisoners and have to rely on their co-operation. Just sometimes, however, the population, or some part of them, decides to withdraw that co-operation, and then everyone is at risk.

There had been a number of escalating incidents over a week with staff being challenged. There were staff shortages which was making it difficult to provide an association period every evening. When you work in a prison for any length of time you can feel when the mood isn't right. On a particular wing one day you could cut the atmosphere with a knife. Word was that if association wasn't granted that evening, the wing would 'go up'. We believed it. We kept back a group of staff after the end of their shift and located them outside the wing, 'kitted up' in Control and Restraint gear.

It was arranged that if the wing 'went up' that evening, staff would yell the imaginative code phrase: *"Send in Mr Blobby!"* (which dates this as Mr Blobby has recently celebrated his 28th birthday) and the stand-by staff would leap in to the rescue. (It was also agreed that if, in the heat of the moment, the code phrase was forgotten and the squad heard: *"Get the Fuck in here"*, or similar, they would not delay.)

I waited with the mustered stand-by staff but the call never came. Encouraged by knowing their colleagues were only a shout away, the wing staff went about their duties confidently and at ease, laughing and joking with their charges. No riot occurred. Perhaps it never would have. Or perhaps the staff's confidence was communicated to the prisoners who decided not to 'play' that night. We'll never know. The atmosphere the rest of the week 'normalised'.

Sometimes working at Aylesbury could be very dangerous.

High up on a landing, Officer Balcombe was grabbed by a prisoner, who held a toothbrush with a blade burnt into it, to his throat. Colleagues nearby instantly and instinctively intervened to grab the prisoner and wrestle him off the Officer. Very luckily, their colleague was not physically hurt.

About a week afterwards I came across Officer Balcombe and asked him how he was. He was very young, only a couple of years older than those in his charge. His eyes were anxious and darted around. Initially restrained, he then became emotional and confessed that he now felt so afraid that he no longer wanted to come to work. He had overwhelming feelings of guilt. In that brief moment when the prisoner had held his life in his hands, the Officer's power had been ripped away from him. He couldn't understand why, when the incident had been so brief and he had suffered no physical injury, he had been affected so deeply.

I remember vividly the first suicide I investigated at Aylesbury.

Marc was nineteen and was transferred in after he had committed a series of assaults in another prison. I interviewed him in the segregation unit following his reception. He had dark hair, glowering eyes, a rather truculent expression, but appeared reconciled to the move. He wouldn't open up except to ask me to remove the name of a family member from his records as his next of kin, refusing to tell me the reason why. He was placed on a normal wing and seemed to settle down into the general population. Just a few weeks later he was dead.

I was asked to investigate because at that time, aside from the Police investigation on behalf of the Coroner, there was no external independent investigation of deaths in custody. Now the Prisons and Probation Ombudsman (PPO) has this task.

Prisoners and staff reported that they hadn't noticed anything really unusual about Marc's behaviour in the days before his death. The only thing someone came up with was, one lunchtime, the wing television had broadcast a news report about the repatriation of soldiers' bodies from a war zone, and when the coffins were carried out of the aircraft's hold, Marc had been seen standing on the centre of the wing, watching and laughing.

I asked the prisoner who lived in the cell opposite Marc's, whether he'd noticed anything unusual the night he had hung himself. He could see a little through the slit in his door frame and through the slit in Marc's door frame opposite.

"He was alright", he said. "He was dancing". I didn't have the heart to tell him what must really have been happening.

Staff also died.

One terrible morning, Albert, an Officer Support Grade supervising a Works contractor, climbed up onto a roof and had a catastrophic heart attack. It took a long time for paramedics to get his body down while colleagues stood below in a shocked, still circle. One volunteered to break the news to Albert's wife and left, head bowed, to drive the few miles necessary. I accompanied Albert's body in the ambulance, staring at his shoes all the way. They were brown.

I ended up being asked to conduct many investigations, some at the far flung ends of the country. I generally enjoyed these. I liked the intellectual exercise of trying to ferret out the truth of what had happened (my detective ambitions hadn't been entirely wasted). But however sensitively managed, there was always pain involved to those affected. Unsurprisingly I didn't get a warm welcome from everyone. Staff would sometimes close ranks and clam up. At one northern gaol the Principal Officer assisting me told me he received a Masonic handshake. No one, for obvious reasons, ever tried that on me.

I was once asked to investigate a temporary release failure from a prison near London. It was a very serious incident because the man concerned had absconded to his home country and almost immediately murdered three people.

Really it should have been a more senior Governor than me investigating because the Governing Governor as required, had approved the release - and I did point this out. Maybe they didn't have one to spare, or perhaps they didn't want the investigation to become too prominent.

The Governor met me briefly on arrival. She was personable, polite, but had a look like a deer caught in the headlights. I felt sorry for her. My conclusion to the investigation was embarrassing. The staff conducting the assessments of the prisoner's risk had been influenced by the Governor. She had let it be known that she wanted this prisoner to be released. They had completed their reports, she had considered the positive recommendations and then authorised the release.

The Governor did not continue in that post for much longer. The prisoner did not return to face the music. At the time of my investigation he remained in his own country on death row.

A year into my time at Aylesbury I was promoted to Governor 4 and inherited the job of 'Head of Inmate Activities'. For the first time I felt able to proudly place a photo of my family on my desk - as in my new impressive office, I was no longer based on a wing with easy access by prisoners.

I took over from an ex-Chief, Mr Sayers, a large contradiction of a man. Befitting tradition he had a no-nonsense manner, was always immaculate in a smart suit, and nothing in his office had been out of place. Unlike the stereotype Chief, he was a fervent vegetarian and a hunt saboteur. Mr Sayers epitomised the label: 'Gate happy'. This is a term used in prisons to describe over excited staff or prisoners approaching release. Mr Sayers had been looking forward to retiring for years and would corner people at any opportunity to describe, at length, all the things he planned to do as soon as he had the time. To be honest, listening to him was tedious, but it gave him a lot of pleasure. He practically leapt out of the prison on his retirement. Tragically, Mr Sayers was to die of a heart attack, less than a year later.

One thing I wanted to do in my new role was increase the number of official Prison Visitors. Official Prison Visitors visit prisoners who rarely, if ever, have visits from friends or family. They are volunteers and are independent of the prison and its staff. We advertised locally.

A very old man was escorted across the yard to my office. He lowered himself with difficulty into the chair. I was worried. There was a piece of paper on my desk with the rules of the scheme, including an official age limit for Prison Visitors of 70. This guy was clearly way past that and I wasn't looking forward to telling him. I made him a cup of tea.

"What made you come to see us today?" I asked. The many lines around the old man's eyes crinkled and he smiled.

"I hoped I might be able to help the boys a little", he said. He proceeded softly and matter-of-factly to tell me something of his history. He had known what it was like to lose one's family, to be imprisoned, to have to travel to a foreign land and start again with nothing. It was as if time had stopped. As we shook hands afterwards I noticed the string of numbers on his arm. I screwed up the piece of paper.

He was a brilliant Prison Visitor.

I enjoyed my struggle to keep our young men occupied. The major problem to tackle was the workshops. We had a TV repair course but unfortunately we only had about four individuals in the entire population ever deemed clever enough to study this. Eventually the instructor who ran the electrical wiring shop retired. Apparently one did not need to be nearly as bright to learn electrical wiring (?) and I eventually persuaded the TV repair shop instructor to take that class on instead. I consider this a major achievement as it took so many, many hours of persuasion.

The other, 'general' workshop was a nightmare. It was staffed by three instructors who regularly put prisoners on report and sent them back to the wings for bad behaviour, and there was plenty of it the place was so hated. This shop was sent 'unskilled' work by the 'Prison Industries' department and there was no attempt at training prisoners in anything useful. Packing socks into boxes was a particular favourite task. I shuddered when I found out one day that we had received an order to pack brake cables. The socks were always being rejected because disgruntled prisoners would shove them into their packaging the wrong way round so you couldn't see the logos. I didn't fancy the idea of brake cables passing through their hands.

Eventually one of the instructors talked about retiring. I didn't try to dissuade him. I used his salary together with some other sequestered resources to plan the introduction of a motor vehicle maintenance training course. This eventually opened after I had left, led by my successor and boosted by sponsorship from Toyota. It was a long struggle, but a significant acquisition for the prison.

Another instructor then departed enabling me to use the funds to set up an Industrial Cleaning course. The only thing I recall about this is the weird delight I experienced helping choose the various permanent floors that would be laid in the little rooms where inmates would practice their cleaning. I can picture some of these still.

Both courses were a lot more popular and meaningful than stuffing socks into boxes.

Special events when we occasionally had enough staff available to supervise them, were always welcomed by our residents. Once in a while theatre groups would offer free productions.

Sometimes what was performed left even me rather baffled but our youngsters appreciated the break from routine and the chance to meet new people, and they were usually well behaved. (We made a point of positioning those most likely to attack each other at opposite ends of the room). The most well received production by far, was a lively interactive play about sexual health. Never was their joy greater when the lead actor rounded on me as the most senior member of staff present, to ask my opinion on anal sex.

My least enamoured responsibility now was the kitchen. I received a call about 8.30am telling me that the gas supply had completely failed and there was no possibility of hot food until it was repaired, and no one had any idea when that was going to happen. The capability of the kitchen wasn't great at the best of times but this was bad.

We got away with sandwiches for lunch but we knew we had to provide a hot meal for tea or risk major trouble. There was no option but to buy-in hot food. We ordered 350 quarter pounders with cheese from Aylesbury McDonald's.

The potential for negative press coverage and inevitable political savaging by our masters was always present. *"On no account do we get Happy Meals!"* Somebody yelled down the corridor. That would definitely not have read well in the tabloids.

I decided to get ahead of the press. I drafted a press release thanking McDonald's sincerely for rising to the challenge and coming to our aid at our time of great crisis. I laid it on a bit thick, but we were genuinely grateful. I then helped cook veggie burgers on the electric cooker in the staff kitchen for the (thankfully) small number of vegetarians we catered for, that at that stage McDonalds didn't. We received no negative press, there was no political backlash and the prisoners enjoyed their unexpected 'treat'. Fortunately, the gas was fixed the next day.

The problems with the kitchen however continued. I had to abandon my previous strategy of eating everything presented to me by unhappy prisoners. There was a limit to my masochism. I spent one lunchtime clad in a white coat behind a heated trolley, assisting wing staff to serve out portions of food (catering staff were always wisely 'too busy' to serve it themselves), cut into the chicken to test it and the raw flesh 'pinged' like elastic. The Senior Officer Caterer shoved it under the grill until it was burnt to a crisp, then sent it back to be re-served.

The Senior Officer Caterer eventually, thankfully, moved on - he was enterprising but he seemed to realise the challenges were too much for him - and I chaired a board for his replacement. We followed usual Civil Service rules, asking the same appropriate questions of each candidate. The Area Catering Manager, who was required to sit on the Board, asked catering questions. (I was pleased to find I knew the correct way to cook boiled potatoes.) I asked questions about leadership and management. To my delight we found an excellent candidate. He was enthusiastic, clearly had management skills and really knew how to cook.

Six weeks later I was informed that my brilliant new addition had been poached by this same Area Catering Manager for his own pet project. Later on the ACM had to deal with me in other circumstances. It was clear that neither of us had forgotten. I confess I was not displeased by how uncomfortable he was in my presence. He knew not to ask me any favours.

There were three Governors in charge while I was at Aylesbury. The first soon moved on - a very ambitious young man. The second was Michael Spurr, on his way to becoming Director General. I enjoyed working with him: I found him a firm but fair consultative leader.

Michael was soon taken to spearhead the latest HQ initiative. Our third Governor was middle aged, with black hair and glasses and a kindly smile. He was very welcome as he was experienced and eager to continue positive change. He was easy to talk to, but I began to get weary of his habit of coming into my office right at the end of the day, wanting to discuss for hours what was on his mind, when I was tired and eager to begin the long drive home. I wasn't aware at the time, but he may have been paddling frantically under the water. After I left Aylesbury he was promoted to govern a much more demanding, high profile prison, but soon had to resign the Service after suffering a mental health crisis triggered by stress.

Stress affects you in strange ways. Senior Officer Marks came to see me. He confided that he would probably need to take sick leave soon, as he had been diagnosed with terminal lung cancer. I was horrified; I was so sorry for him and his family. He was a popular man too and his colleagues were devastated. Mr Marks kept working and remained well. Months later I asked his permission to write to his doctor, to ask about appropriate duties to deploy him to long-term. I duly wrote a letter but received a very woolly reply. I assumed that the doctor was being cagey because of medical confidentiality. I wrote again, reminding him I had his patient's permission for disclosure but the same thing occurred. Eventually I rang the doctor.

The next day I called Mr Marks into my office. I sat him down, took a breath and informed him that he did not have lung cancer and was not going to die. He looked at me blankly. It took some time to persuade him. The doctor, it turned out, had mentioned something to him about growths on his lungs - probably harmless old tuberculosis scars. The Senior Officer had somehow completely misinterpreted what he had said and presumably had been too frightened to go back and see him again. It felt good, but very strange, to be able to break the news to someone that they were going to live. I remembered a prisoner about to have his world ended as he walked into an office to see John Marriott and the prison doctor in Aylesbury.

Prisons were now being threatened with 'market testing'. This meant for the gaol concerned, the management team supported by the unions, had to demonstrate that they could produce significant cost savings and improve delivery. The threat was, if they failed to make a convincing case, the prison would be handed over to be run by the private sector and the staff would transfer to the new employer. Our political masters were demanding public sector prisons be as cheap to run as the new private sector prisons. It was, however, an unrealistic demand. Staff at private prisons were poorer paid. Public sector staff were on different terms and conditions and it would take years to be able to recruit enough new staff on less favourable terms, to be competitive. There were of course consequences for private prisons too: staffing prisons with poorer paid staff with no experience led to many incidents. The turnover of private sector staff was very high.

One day we received a short and devastating missive from HQ informing us that Aylesbury was now on the list for market testing. We were angry and frustrated as it felt like a kick in the teeth for all our hard work. During the course of the day a spirit of defiance came over us and we marched out of the prison that night singing *'Always Look on the Bright Side of Life'*, with particular emphasis on the swear words.

As a reward for making the list we attracted some high profile visitors. One of these was the then Home Secretary Michael Howard. The prison Principal Psychologist and I waited in the Governor's secretary's office to be introduced to him. It was long past lunchtime, we still hadn't been summoned, and we were hungry. The only thing prisoners on the catering course could be relied upon to make without disaster, was chocolate eclairs. There was an impressive pyramid of them a-waiting our guest. By the time we were summoned in, the pile was considerably smaller. We had been creative in our efforts to rearrange them as we ate.

Michael Howard had an intense stare and a snake-like charm. He leaned forward, gazed into my eyes and asked if I had any ideas for publicly acceptable community service alternatives to prison. This was then a hot topic in the tabloids.

Put on the spot, I suddenly recalled an episode of Frasier I'd seen in which Roz had litter-picked by the side of the road. The offenders had worn high visibility jackets clearly stating why they were doing, what they were doing. I described this vision. Not long afterwards, the issue of hi vis jackets for offenders undertaking community service was to be the subject of a major row between the Probation Service and the Government. Probation staff didn't want the jackets to label those on community service as 'offenders' for fear that they would attract abuse and attack by members of the public, and the politicians did. Some say this led to the Government's determination to bring the Probation Service down. I have had a horrible feeling ever since that I may have been responsible for this.

As we expected, the Sword of Damocles which was 'market testing', did nothing to ease the day to day challenges we had running the gaol. It didn't enable us to deliver more for less, or improve the cooperation we had from the unions, but did give us a massive extra headache and an awful lot more paperwork. Eventually and thankfully, we fell off the list again after the selection criteria for the unlucky contenders changed.

By February 1994, I was pregnant again. Life with our second offspring was always destined to be entertaining. I threw up in the car park in full view of the CCTV cameras. Heavily pregnant, I skidded on mud left by a tractor, wrote off a small bridge and landed the car at right angles in a ditch. I also developed a weird craving for the smell of leather and old books. Luckily my office was opposite a little staff room which was stuffed full of ancient magazines; it was my favourite place.

One morning in October, after a dramatically short labour, Daughter Number Two announced her arrival. She would screw up her face and turn alarmingly bright red when she screamed but was otherwise delightful. After three months I returned to work and had to explain what a breast pump was to the pink faced Officer Support Grade operating the X-ray machine.

I absolutely loved working at Aylesbury; it was my favourite posting. But after four years it was time to move on.

Chapter 8: The New Prison

HMP Brockhill, Worcestershire, 2004

I slowly take a sip of my tea. It is peaceful here. The Director is looking at me. He speaks quietly: "If you want your allegations to be investigated I have to tell you there are likely to be repercussions. Your life could become very difficult". He pauses. "But it's up to you."
I don't take long to decide.

HMP Woodhill, Milton Keynes, 1997-1998

I joined HMP Woodhill when I was 35 years old. For the first time in eighteen years we had a Labour Government and golden daffodils were blooming in the hedgerows. I was excited and optimistic about taking on a new challenge.

Woodhill was a very different sort of prison. Built in the 1990s it held around eight hundred male prisoners of all categories, adults and young men, in innovatively designed buildings. Wings were galleried but one-sided and each looked out onto an open expanse of windows which made the units light and less claustrophobic than usual. The only slight disadvantage of this design was that the landings did not allow a net to be strung between them and so prisoners would occasionally take a header off them, or assist their neighbours to do so.

The Governing Governor of this edifice was one of the first women Governing Governors running a male prison. She was quiet, cerebral and astute.

There were three other Governor 4s at Woodhill besides me. I didn't take to one. He had a bushy black beard and a habit of putting his arm around my shoulders and squeezing me tightly when he thought I needed to know something. I found this patronising as he didn't do it to the men. Besides his beard scratched. The second one was a really nice guy, the father of twins and popular with everyone. The third, to my surprise, turned out to have trained as a priest alongside my father-in-law many years earlier. These three were strong characters. They ran competing empires within the establishment and commanded and usually received loyalty.

I was initially made 'Head of Residential' which meant I was responsible for the running of the accommodation wings. At this time there were already Governor 5s and Principal Officers in charge of these units and I soon realised the function was vastly over-managed. Indeed, after a later reorganisation, the 'Head of Residential' post was removed. I tried to think creatively and find things to do, but there was a limit to how often I could patrol the landings, Sergeant-Major like, drinking tea with the troops, without any actual work to get stuck into. Except for the tasks required when I was Duty Governor, I was bored rigid. Luckily the post of 'Head of Operations' soon opened up. The person in this job was primarily responsible for security. It was an important post particularly in this prison, a challenge, and I hadn't done it before. I eagerly begged for and was given the job.

I immediately took to my new role: *'Head of Macho Things'* as I quietly christened it, like a fish to water. There was plenty going on. Woodhill was soon to take Category A prisoners and there were major concerns as to whether the place was up to scratch. I set out to learn the minutiae of all my responsibilities: the Security Department, the Dog Section, the Intelligence System, the Emergency Control Room, the Visits Complex and the Gate. It was all strangely fascinating. I visited the kennels, explored the darkest recesses of the buildings, watched as staff stuck probes down drains, and had many long discussions. I spent weeks writing and rewriting contingency plans and Operational Instructions.

This was the time when money was available to improve security. To reflect its high security status as a 'Core Local' prison, Woodhill was awarded extra cash to create a 'Dedicated Search Team'. Concern had arisen that some staff were being 'conditioned' by the prisoners they looked after, to ignore the security threat that they posed. The 'DST' would be a group of staff whose sole job would be to search prisoners and areas of the prison. Based away from the wings, it was hoped these staff would not be under the same conditioning influence. Moreover, such a team would have more time to search, than wing staff who had to find time alongside other duties.

The existence of this new Dedicated Search Team meant more searching was done. But there were some negative consequences. As well as their searching duties, the team were available to respond to incidents. There began to be allegations made about 'excessive use of force' by the staff. There was suspicion that a couple of the DST were enjoying this aspect of their duties a little too much. Uniforms that we had kitted the staff out in were dark green, and soon prisoners began referring to the team as the 'Green Shirts'. There was an uncomfortable whiff of the stormtrooper around. Fortunately perhaps, the

DST did not last long: funding was pulled to save costs.

As Head of Operations I was often being presented with potential security threats. One such was an allegation that a nurse was having an affair with an inmate. The prisoner was working as an orderly in the prison hospital and was on remand charged with the rape of his partner.

Mindful that some male staff were deeply prejudiced against women working in their prisons, I regarded the allegation with a degree of suspicion. There was little evidence, merely two people lingering 'a little too long' in a storeroom together. To protect the woman from further rumours however, I moved the prisoner, Dowds, out of the prison hospital. He took it well when I told him. A dark-haired and personable young man, obviously under strain, he knew that he was powerless to object.

Nurse Williams was angry: she had a mass of brown curls which she tossed back indignantly.

"It's not fair on him. Why should he lose his job? He's done nothing wrong." I assured her we weren't judging him and he wouldn't be damaged by the allegation. He was a hard worker and would soon get a good job on his new wing. The move was made and I thought nothing more of it.

Many months after I had left Woodhill I met some staff from the prison. They mentioned that Dowds had been released and the nurse had left the Service. They were living together.

Prisoners should never be underestimated. A man was found dead in the hospital wing, obviously having taken his own life. I spoke to the prisoner in the cell next to him and found myself physically repelled by him. Adams was huge and fleshy like a massive doughy baby. As a result of the suicide Adams was now understandably extremely vulnerable. We kept him on 'intermittent watch'[10] for a long time and he was given a good deal of support.

---

10 Where the prisoner is checked at random times.

About a year afterwards I discovered Adams had been transferred to a London prison where a few months later his next door neighbour too, had killed himself. Following investigation by the Police of that tragedy and the re-investigation of several others, Adams was charged with inciting the suicide of three prisoners, including ours at Woodhill.

We had plenty of other incidents of course, as usual often food related. One lunchtime I was informed that all the prisoners on a wing had declined their meal, and were now refusing to be 'banged up'. I was in the vicinity so went onto the wing and started talking to them. I did not feel threatened as the mood was calm, but it crossed my mind suddenly that I could easily be taken hostage. It was a real possibility. As perimeter security was improving and roofs were being made less easy to climb, there was speculation then that hostage taking by frustrated or desperate prisoners was bound to increase. Afterwards it occurred to me to give Rob a list of instructions on what to do if he ever got that message. Not to tell my parents would be No.1 on my list.

I liked being Duty Governor responding to incidents. I did not enjoy night visits though, which were a requirement for everyone, once a month. These involved a return to the prison in the wee small hours and took forever. You did not carry keys so you were escorted by the Night Orderly Officer (at Woodhill this was a Principal Officer) and a dog handler. It was good to meet the staff and have a chat but it was shattering, especially after a day's work and a long drive.

Nowhere is as silent as a prison at night. Looming buildings. Hundreds of men for a moment muted. Only the pad pad pad of footsteps. Occasionally you meet a patrol, pass a low greeting, move on. Silence engulfs you. Suddenly, an ear splitting crash as keys hit lock and a gate shrieks open. And then the pad pad pad begins again.

I grew into my new role and enjoyed the authority I now had, operating within this challenging place. I took every chance to upskill myself including training in how to command hostage incidents and I sometimes helped out with the training of negotiators. I attended an event with the local Police Commander. The fundamental difference in our approaches was clear: "It's our natural instinct to contain perpetrators, to lock them down", I explained to him.

He replied, "Ours is to bring them out into the open, expose them and shoot them".

Not that I never made mistakes of course. One cold winter's evening when I was Duty Governor, just when darkness was falling, the whole of the perimeter lighting suddenly failed. This was serious. Power may have been cut deliberately to 'spring' a prisoner, or if not, this was an excellent chance for opportunistic escape attempts. While Works staff fought to get the standby generators going, having ordered the prison to be locked down, I sent dog handlers to circle the exterior of the gaol, and, cleverly as I thought, deployed the PE Instructors with torches to 'Fixed Posts' (pre-assigned positions within the prison) to spot any men attempting to make a break for the wall. Around four hours later the generator was finally kicked into life and I stood the PEIs down. They were frozen rigid. It might have been an idea to send them out wearing coats, not just shorts and vests.

My other life continued. Daughter No 2's christening had been another wonderful day full of cake and chat in the rectory garden in Norfolk. My dad had however arrived alone. My mum, he said, had refused to leave the house and he hadn't been able to persuade her. In a way of course, like the wedding, it was a relief. Her mood was usually stable at the few events like these she attended but I was never sure what odd remarks she might make or how she might behave and I was always on edge. I would feel protective towards her but also shame.

After we returned home dumping children and the torrents of accompanying baby support equipment in the hall, the phone was already ringing. My father sounded bewildered: "She isn't here," he said. "I've waited ages but she hasn't come back".

My mother would sometimes disappear but not for long - just enough to worry us. Occasionally my dad would be summoned by the police to collect her. This was the longest she had been missing.

It took me under 15 minutes ringing round to locate her. She had called an ambulance almost immediately after my father had left for the christening. When the paramedics arrived she appeared mute and hardly able to walk.

When I entered the ward at Brighton General Hospital several hours later I had a flashback to a previous visit. I was about 11 and sitting by my mother's bedside. She was screaming at me and a nurse came up and patted me on the arm. This time my mother was silent and would not meet my eyes.

"We can't find any physical cause", the doctor murmured. We both knew what he meant.

I looked down at my dad. He seemed tiny. Always very thin he was now a wisp of himself. I had no idea how he would cope any longer or how we could help him from so far away. But the doctor was still speaking: "We think your mum needs full time care…".

We moved my mother from Brighton to a pleasant nursing home by the river in Abingdon, so we could easily visit her, and my father put the family home on the market. Dad moved in with us, living initially in a makeshift bedroom we had created for him out of our dining room. With most of the proceeds from the house my father bought my mum an annuity which would pay for her care.

The arrangement worked out. Mum seemed to be pleased to see us when we visited; it was harder than ever to tell what was going through her mind though, as she rarely spoke. We bribed the kids with a stop-off at McDonalds and at the nursing home they entertained themselves by turning somersaults on an upholstered pouffe in the lounge to the delight of some of the residents.

Dad spent the rest of the money from the house sale on funding the building of a self-contained annex to our house for him to live in, but he never got to occupy it. My mother had now released him from the burden of caring for her but perhaps the release itself was too great a shock, or simply too late.

Together with his diabetes and Parkinsons, he began to display symptoms of Lewy Body dementia. It was very tough on Rob looking after him while I was at work, as well as caring for the kids who couldn't be expected to understand what was happening. I worried a lot. On very bad days I used to cry on the way to work: it was the only time available.

My dad went into respite care, then broke his thigh, his symptoms of dementia became extreme and eventually he ended up living in a nursing home in Chipping Norton.

The illness brought interesting hallucinations, luckily not usually distressing. Often they involved children or cats, both of which he loved. Sometimes they were more bizarre. Once he told us he'd been visited by the Home Secretary and they had discussed how best to run the country. We patted him on the shoulder and took him out for a cream tea.

Much later I discovered that the home lay in Douglas Hurd's constituency and he had popped in for a visit.

Dad was never defeated. He was an expert amateur archaeologist and had been chair of the Brighton & Hove Archaeology Society. Much of my childhood had been spent with him and my mother (when well), scraping up long-lost civilisations in various fields and ditches around the Sussex countryside. Now he acquired some old maps from somewhere and deduced that in the surrounding area there should be traces of an ancient fortification. Then he tramped through the local woods until he found it. The proprietor of the home confessed afterwards that he had badgered them until they had let him out by himself. They probably expected him to nip down the shops to buy a paper.

Work was a welcome distraction during those days. I had shared what was happening at home with the Nice Guy and the Priest and I was grateful for their quiet support. I didn't, however, tell my boss, the Deputy Governor.

The Deputy Governor when I arrived at Woodhill was a formidable man. Everyone, including me, was not a little afraid of him, but everybody including me, admired him. He resembled the revered Chief of the past but he was no stereotype. He was physically large, but clever, aware of both his own strengths and the areas he needed to leave to others in these changing times. Two years after my arrival at Woodhill he was promoted to his own Governing Governor's post.

At his leaving party he stood up and solemnly announced that he would like to recite a poem. We stood in respectful silence. It was Baldrick's from 'Blackadder Goes Forth': "Boom boom boom boom, boom boom boom boom, boom boom boom boom...."

The man who took over from the 'Chief' could not have been more of a contrast to him. He was short, slight, very quiet and vaguely resembled a Dickensian bank clerk. The Governor asked me what I thought of him. "He seems nice". I said tentatively.

"I hope he's a lot more than that", she snapped back.

A few months later there were opportunities to apply for promotion. The Clerk refused to tick the box endorsing my application. I was stunned. Refusing to endorse someone's application for promotion wasn't done unless there was a bloody good reason. I had been in my current grade for four years at two establishments, learned a lot, worked hard, sorted out many complex issues and had managed some very difficult situations. I asked him the reason for his decision. The Clerk hesitated then mumbled that he thought I should have been content with staying as Head of Residential rather than asking to move to Operations. I struggled to make sense of that. Since when was ambition and a desire to take on more challenging work a fault? I asked him to explain what he meant but he wouldn't give me an answer.

As Head of Operations I now commanded significant authority within the prison. The Clerk was himself newly promoted and as Deputy Governor, the only people he had working directly to him were four stroppy Governor 4s and we wielded the real power. As I saw it the Clerk, not naturally assertive, knew he had a massive hill to climb if he was to prove to the staff that he was anything like as credible as the old 'Chief'. I believed he was consciously (or unconsciously) trying to take me down a peg or two and assert himself.

I went to the Governor who looked sympathetic. She said she would talk to the Clerk, went to see him, returned and told me: "I'm sorry but he's sticking by his decision". She wasn't going to overrule her deputy. I felt let down but I wasn't surprised.

Mule-headed, I decided to sit the Board anyway, as I was technically still allowed to do, so sure I was that I was qualified and deserved to be there. In retrospect I'm surprised now that I had the arrogance (or confidence?) to do that. On the day I was nervous but answered questions well I think, but I wasn't successful. So presumably they didn't think I was suitable for promotion either. Or maybe I was naive to attend and sunk by my manager's non-endorsement before I had entered the room.

A few weeks passed and I realised working for the Clerk was no longer viable. I had lost what respect I had had for him and some of the joy had gone from my job. What was even more of a problem now was, the Clerk appeared very nervous whenever he had to deal with me. I didn't think working for someone who was frightened of me was going to be much fun going forward, for either of us.

I had worked at Woodhill for less than two years but I began looking around for jobs. The Area Manager needed a new Staff Officer. I applied.

Chapter 9: The Bag Carrier

HMP Brockhill, Worcestershire, 2003

A young prisoner, Dana, kills herself. The wing howls with grief. Flowers are laid in her cell and cards are written. The Chaplain holds a special service in the dining room on the wing. Most people come to pay their respects, and everyone cries. With her families' consent, we plant a tree in the prison garden in her memory. A little memorial for a life.

Chilterns Prison Service Area Office, London, 1998-2000

I became Staff Officer to the Chilterns Area Manager when I was 36. I would probably have taken the first post I could to get out of Woodhill at that point, but I did like the idea of doing something completely different for a while. Not that I really understood all the job entailed. All I knew was, Staff Officers were the right hand assistants to the Area Managers, based with their teams in Cleland House, a rather dilapidated office block near Lambeth Bridge, London. All the Area Offices were together on two floors and each was run by a team of mainstream civil servants with the Staff Officer (i.e. me) (theoretically) in charge.

The Executive Officer, Sheena (who really ran the office) was wise and reliable and had seen many Staff Officers come and go. She was placid, appearing mildly amused on the surface. Only occasionally would she show a touch of irritation. She suffered, I suspected, seeing others a little luckier and a little flashier progress more quickly up the Civil Service tree.

A series of agency staff were employed to fill vacant assistant posts, one of whom, Sasha, had black hair and nails and if you asked her anything would glare fiercely at you for some seconds before deigning to reply. We were all slightly scared of her. Unwisely, I thought, the team brought her a set of kitchen knives as a parting gift when she left.

My favourite gift to us from the agency though, was an Administrative Assistant I christened the Great Dane. He was young, blonde, charming and made me laugh. Although sometimes a little annoying, and occasionally misguided, he nearly always brightened my day. Every office should have one. He called me "Bab-era" and I still miss him a little.

One of our biggest difficulties was keeping our Area Manger - Jeremy - in personal secretaries: he went through dozens. He probably wasn't the problem. I don't think we paid the agency enough to get a good one.

Jeremy was a tall, dapper, clever man with a quietly cheeky sense of humour. He had been a pilot in the RAF in a previous life. I tried to picture him operating the controls of a plane but I struggled: he couldn't even work the photocopier.

Jeremy was absolutely dedicated to his work. He was particularly interested in supporting the children of prisoners and became a hard-working patron of a national charity. He had the annoying habit, however, of getting involved with and trying to solve every single issue that crossed his path, however unconnected with our day-to-day business.

The daily post used to arrive in a massive flurry of brown treasury envelopes like leaf fall in autumn. Emails were yet to become the all dominating form of communication that they are now. At first this wasn't a problem as I couldn't read Jeremy's handwriting and I had misinterpreted *"PI deal"* on everything as: *"I'll deal"*. It was a nasty shock when I realised the truth. For a few weeks I struggled to keep up. Fortunately a solution soon became clear. As well as being clever Jeremy was also one of the most absent minded people I've ever met and rarely remembered anything he asked me to do. I started tackling what I thought was important and 'filed' the rest.

Jeremy regularly brought all his Governors together and we took turns to meet at their various prisons. It was interesting to see how different people operated. Some would relax among colleagues and admit to stress and seek support. One, a lovely man, worryingly struggled to even chair a discussion. I couldn't imagine how he could cope with his POA. A few would put up a bit of a tough front. A couple were simply brilliant individuals. One of these left quickly for an accelerated career in the Home Office - a big loss to the Prison Service I thought. For another newly promoted Governor his responsibilities almost instantly proved too much. He disappeared suddenly from his post after weeks of failing to sleep.

There was a lot of laughter, some resolution of mutual problems, and occasionally a little learning. Jeremy had the bright idea of bringing in some outside speakers in an attempt to inspire people. One was a round little man with a white beard who looked rather wild. He gave us a lecture on Leadership.

"Why is it", he said jabbing his finger at us, "That some people can get others to wrap explosives around themselves and blow themselves up, yet we struggle to persuade Betty in admin to do a bit of extra photocopying".

Whenever I felt I was beating my head against a brick wall trying to get people to do things in years to come, those words would come back to haunt me.

From time to time other Governor grades would be attached to the team.

One, Bob, was a senior Works manager. His moment came during the Year 2000 preparations. None of us really believed Doomsday loomed but boy, did the Service prepare! There were all sorts of theories about how every kind of technology would fall apart as the clock struck midnight, because computer calendars were not constructed to last beyond 1999. Many many meetings had been held to plan contingencies. Our man spent the night before the fateful day in a deserted lay-by at the wheel of a large truck with a standby generator ready to dash, like Superman, to the rescue of our prisons. Frustratingly, possibly, no call ever came.

Another attached to the team for a while was a very keen Governor 5. Whippet-like he was full of energy and not a little frustrated, as his natural home was not an office. Once, the Whippet came into his own. We were advised by Special Branch that some heavy criminals were planning to spring a prisoner imminently from one of our gaols. They thought it possible that keys might have been obtained to effect the escape, but were adamant that no one at all on staff, including the Governor, was to be informed that 'information had been received'. This posed a quandary. Clearly the prison needed to be re-locked and quickly.

Co-incidentally, members of our team were due to visit the place the next day. The Whippet toured the prison escorted by an Officer. He had made a crude drawing from memory of a key and when the Officer looked away for a second he threw it on the ground. Shortly afterwards, a white faced Governor was seen to run out of his office, the Whippet's drawing in hand. The Governor's request for a re-lock was, of course, sympathetically received.

"And do you know", the Whippet told me afterwards, "I had to drop the bloody thing three times before the bloody Officer noticed it".

My new role was interesting. I was learning a lot from observing our Governors and listening to Jeremy. He was very open with me about his concerns and frustrations. Sometimes Governors would ask me what I thought Jeremy's attitude would be about something; I would tell them, and they wouldn't bother him. Or a sheepish Governor would ring to confess some minor disaster and then ask me to break the news. Occasionally I had delusions of megalomania and felt I was running the Area. At one point Jeremy left the country for six weeks trusting me to keep the place ticking over. I think I only once needed to contact the Governor he had left as my go-to person for advice.

The Service was then experimenting with new types of management training and some of us Staff Officers were sent off for a weekend. We were given coloured markers and large sheets of paper and encouraged to draw cathartically and quickly how we saw our role in our organisation. Imaginations became very Medieval, dragons and castles predominating. I began to portray my role as gatekeeper for the office and for Jeremy. I was no knight on horseback though. When my artistic effort was displayed to the room I discovered to my horror that I had drawn a giant womb. The staff and Jeremy were happy embryos. I was the cervix.

As time went by, rather to my surprise, I found that I enjoyed working in an office. I liked the trivialities that made the day pass. In those ancient days there was a tea trolley that sailed the corridors twice a day - with cakes! It was a little joyful moment to break the routine.

We had fun and laughed a lot. For a few months I took tap dancing lessons in the evenings and would demonstrate my latest moves up and down the office, no doubt to everyone's embarrassment, but they put up with it.

At Christmas, we decorated. I went to TOWN. Entering the outer office, people were forced to plough their way through densely hanging tinsel and baubles in order to find their way to Jeremy's room. The team named it *'Barbara's Bordello'*.

We had a 'word of the day' which was inscribed on the whiteboard. We tried to put this into everything we wrote. It was a challenge to get it into high-level briefings.

Opening our front door one morning, bracing myself for the daily rush to the railway station, I encountered our next door neighbour's elderly dog, Blue. He was a beautiful gentle old thing and I bent down to speak to him. As I did so there was a flurry of movement and I felt a blinding crack of agony across my forehead, then blood began trickling down my face. I was unaware Blue's trick was to leap up and 'kiss' you. I had to give up any idea of catching my train and worked from home. I learned later that on that day, the whiteboard in the office had read, in very large letters for all to see:

BARBARA TREEN SICK
HEAD-BUTTED BY OLD BLIND DOG
WE ARE SO WORRIED

It wasn't quite as exciting as working in a prison. I did once get stuck in a lift, though. The patient man I was trapped with (for three hours) was remarkably understanding given that I had caused it by dropping my Tesco's Clubcard down the crack in the doorframe.

We had one other break in the routine. The building opposite was being renovated and regularly caught fire. We would all stream out of the building, sunbathe on the grass in the park opposite and lazily make deals between ourselves before reluctantly drifting back.

My father's health deteriorated further and eventually he slipped away peacefully one quiet summer morning while I was reading to him. My mother died in her sleep of pneumonia six months later.

When I rang my father's friends to inform him of his death I promised them that later I would try to arrange a proper memorial service in Brighton for him, but in my heart of hearts I knew I probably wouldn't do it. I had too little energy and too much grief.

I wrote and read the eulogies at both the brief funerals Rob and I arranged for my parents. I spoke with pride of my father's achievements: as a Chartered Electrical Engineer, as an archaeologist and of his time in the Home Guard during the war. At my mother's funeral I didn't allow my complex feelings towards her to spill out. Pity, anger and grief at the loss of a loving relationship that we would now never have, remained walled up. I did hint though, at the troubled times I suspected she had experienced in her youth, as some explanation for how she was. But the truth was I knew little. It wasn't something we dared to ask her about. Anything that risked bringing about an emotional state - like memories of her little brothers or sisters, or early life with my father, or playing music - was risky. Her mood might suddenly veer into depression, then hours of rage. I didn't mention at the funeral that I suspected she had experienced abuse. She had once remarked, out of the blue, that she used to sleep with a knife under her pillow. I regret that I didn't get to know the person she was meant to be: the beautiful, hopeful young woman, proudly wearing her nurse's uniform, in the black and white photograph on my bookcase.

I have been asked whether my experience of living with a mother who was mentally ill, made me somehow more empathetic and able to understand vulnerable prisoners - particularly women. I guess the answer is maybe 'yes,' but I would forever feel a failure for not being able to better understand and empathise with her, even when I was an adult. Too much damage had been done.

My mother's ashes I sprinkled in the garden of remembrance at Brighton crematorium. Following my father's wishes, my friend Elizabeth and I climbed up onto the South Downs one windy morning and together we scattered his ashes in that beautiful place he loved best. The wind turned, a speck of ash went in my eye and I started laughing. It felt like dad was teasing me, reminding me that he was never leaving me.

As time went on commuting began proving a strain. Life both at work and at home was demanding and I wasn't getting much sleep.

Home was a release, but there was little time to relax. Each night small children would hit me like loving missiles as I came through the door. As they clung to me, I would fight to get out of my suit before any of the Billy Bear ham and tinned spaghetti Rob had fed them for lunch decided to re-emerge. And although I did not now have to work weekends even these, as every parent knows, were not stress-free.

One Sunday while Rob held the fort, I stole half an hour in between domestic duties for a precious bath. My bubbly coma came to an abrupt end after I heard giggling and opened my eyes only to discover Daughter Number Two, now aged 4, had let a small neighbour in to play and was giving her a tour of the house with Yours Truly as the first exhibit.

Work, although enjoyable, was relentless. Travelling to and fro with one's boss most days didn't help as I couldn't switch off. We talked incessantly about the issues besetting the Area. The migraines I'd suffered with since a small child began hitting me frequently. These migraines 'with aura' involve a period of disturbed vision, inability to talk and most worryingly, briefly affect my ability to understand what I am observing. Then the pain takes over. I began to get frightened about this happening in public places, where I wouldn't be able to control the situation.

Once I had a migraine on a tube just before it broke down at Oxford Circus. I fought my way out and up to street level, and somehow flagged down a taxi. I managed to tell the cabbie to take me to Marylebone as my bewildered brain thought the word sounded familiar. I climbed into a train destined for Stratford upon Avon, pretty sure that wasn't where I lived, but it sounded like it was a good place to be. My reason returned en route but I felt terrible and I was ill for several days.

I had another migraine on the train with Jeremy. He had been busy discussing some problem or other with me. I had been due to attend Daughter Number Two's dance show that evening. That was a very low moment. There was, and usually is, a short time of clarity and angry grief, before the brain clouds over. I growled at him how I would now be spending what was to be a happy night, disappointed and in pain. I was to feel a little safer when I started carrying a card that I could show to people to explain what was happening to me when I got an attack. I would never use it. But I knew it was there.

After I had served two and a half years in Chilterns Area Office I accepted that the migraines weren't going to get any less frequent unless I stopped commuting. An intriguing secondment opportunity near our home came up and I applied.

Chapter 10: The Partnership

HMP Brockhill, Worcestershire, 2003

A small girl, aged about 7 or 8, is climbing down the stone steps from the visits room. She is clutching in her hand the string of a balloon someone had given her. The balloon floats high in the air above her, an incongruous splash of colour against the grey. She is weeping.

The Thames Valley Partnership, 2000-2002

I joined the Thames Valley Partnership in Spring 2000. I was 38. The TVP is a crime prevention charity and was set up by a group of statutory agencies in 1993, to try to produce some innovative solutions to crime and disorder problems in Buckinghamshire, Oxfordshire and Berkshire.

Originally I found myself sharing an office in a redundant police station in Thame, Oxfordshire, but shortly after my arrival, the Partnership moved offices to a beautiful barn conversion on top of the

Chiltern hills. We were surrounded by fields of horses and cattle and the views were stunning. There was a touch of magic about that place. No one believed me, but I swear I witnessed a cow limbo under a fence. We even had use of a little outside swimming pool, but only my kids were crazy enough to try the bracing water.

There was a national blockade of petrol stations during this time by farmers, threatening a shortage of fuel. When it struck, on a mad impulse, inspired by the beauty around me, I acquired a second-hand bike and cycled to work. I hadn't cycled for years and the hills and distance nearly killed me: there was no question of cycling back home again. Rob came to my rescue in the car accompanied by two giggling children. The bike went in the boot, and then permanently into the garage.

With me at the Partnership were three Probation Officers, two Police Sergeants and two Social Workers as well as support staff. My career up to this point had been varied and exciting but now I was stepping way out of my comfort zone. There was a definite moment of: *"What the hell am I doing here*?" Later I was told that everyone joining the Partnership had exactly the same thought.

I quickly settled in and got to know the team. I soon realised that I was on pretty much the same wavelength as my Police Officer colleagues and I understood where Probation were coming from too. The Social Workers, though, seemed to think in a different and interesting way. We all enjoyed discussing our contrasting worlds and we all came together as a team to collaborate, sharing a passion for what we were doing.

I became particularly close to Police Sergeant Katy. She was warm and wise, and appeared to have a borderline stalking obsession for Kevin Spacey. Those were the days of course, before his downfall.

The male Police Sergeant, James, was forever being drawn into dealing with incidents, even though he was not on operational duties. In my early days there we noticed on our CCTV that a young man was climbing in over our back gate, presumably intent on a little petty theft. James was deep in a report. He sighed, took off his jacket and pulled out his warrant card.

Another day, James came into work with a large plaster on his arm. The night before he had been having a quiet meal in a restaurant with his partner when a fight had kicked off outside. One individual seemed to be getting the worst of it, so reluctantly James had put down his pizza and gone out to intervene. The attackers fled leaving the man on the ground. James went to pick him up, but the ungrateful so-and-so promptly bit him. James had the foresight to drag his assailant, the man's teeth still clenched determinedly down on his arm, up to the nearest CCTV, where James shoved his arm and both their faces into view of the camera. He knew how vital it is to preserve evidence.

There was a wide range of interesting work going on. It included a drama project about domestic violence, youth art projects and research into the trauma caused by child abuse.

A race awareness project had been underway in schools using a children's novel as a focus. This was *The Heartstone Odyssey* by Arvan Kumar. The story is about the hope of triumph over race hate and is told through the eyes of a girl who longs to dance. It also features elephants, swans, a porcupine and some astronomer mice. The book is wonderful and made a big impression on me.

I was given a number of tasks.

One was to conduct a review of community safety projects carried out over three years, involving the Britwell Estate in Slough. Much money had been spent trying to improve life for residents and the area's Community Safety Officer wanted to discover why some projects had succeeded and others failed.

I learned some useful lessons which were to serve me well later. Projects succeeded when firm foundations were laid and proper consultation was done. They succeeded when communities' strengths were understood and recognised, wheels were not reinvented, local people led and delivered services and the media were managed.

Projects failed due to over-reliance on information technology and naivety about the length of time it takes to design and install it. They failed when projects relied completely on key individuals who might disappear. They failed due to poor research, particularly when it did not assess likely take-up (as opposed to need). They failed due to poor on-going evaluation and having no exit strategy.

Those I interviewed felt that there were other factors at work however. One was the selective education system. Only a tiny handful of children ever made it into the grammar school from the estate and even less made it to further education. I have always been an opponent of selective education and this cemented my view.

I was also given the lead in the team for mentally disordered offenders (MDOs). A variety of schemes existed in the Thames Valley to divert MDO's from police stations and courts into mental health services. Progress was slow and the prisons were overcrowded. One of the reasons for this was, and is, that so many people have both mental health and substance misuse issues. Having this 'dual diagnosis' usually excluded someone from critical services they needed, like accommodation. People would end up homeless, disconnected from health services and often involved in crime.

I was particularly impressed by a charity called Revolving Doors. They would stick by their clients and would not expect them to undertake complicated journeys to their office like so many agencies, but search them out, finding them on park benches if necessary, and support them in managing the basics like budgeting and negotiating with the landlord.

Of particular concern for prison staff was the time it took getting a prisoner transferred to hospital. Even when diagnosed as having a serious, treatable mental illness prisoners could wait for weeks. If someone was diagnosed with a Personality Disorder the situation was even more dire: no treatment of any kind was offered[11]. Prison Officers felt inadequately trained to care for so many seriously ill people, whom everyone agreed should not be in prison in the first place.

All of us in the Partnership were involved in promoting Restorative Justice. RJ involves repairing the harm caused by a crime, both to victims and the wider community. Our criminal justice system, in contrast, is almost entirely about one thing - retribution. RJ has been around since prehistory and exists in some form in most countries and cultures. It is a broad term

11 Studies have estimated that, whilst Personality Disorder affects between 4-11% of the UK population, its prevalence in the criminal justice system is far higher: 60-70% of prisoners and about 50% of offenders managed by providers of probation services. (Working with offenders with personality disorder A practitioner's guide, National Offenders Management Service and NHS 2015).

encompassing all kinds of mediation and conflict resolution. I was impressed by the healing and relief victims and communities can experience when the process is done well.

I met many different practitioners, including some mediators who had worked in Northern Ireland and some with South Africa's Truth and Reconciliation Commission. They were such modest and courageous people. I thought if they can bring about some peace in the face of such hatred surely I can learn something about RJ and use it in my career.

I learned RJ is not the answer to everything. I read how John Braithwaite, a famous RJ practitioner, described potential subjects for RJ in terms of a pyramid. The bottom section of the pyramid contains people who are both 'rational' and 'virtuous': RJ should work with them. The next section up the pyramid contains a smaller group, although still rational, these people are not virtuous. RJ will not work with them and their anti-social behaviour can only be affected through deterrence (installing in them some fear of consequences). The peak of the pyramid contains the few people who are neither virtuous nor rational. RJ will not work with them either. If you cannot get rid of them, your only choice is to put them somewhere where they can do the least damage. This resonated with me: with prisoners, it was the segregation unit. With staff, it was the Gate.

I was given responsibility within the team for promoting RJ within the Thames Valley prisons. There had been a long but limited history of RJ schemes in gaols. These had usually been arranged through probation services, the chaplaincy or volunteers where either victim-offender mediation had been facilitated at the request of victims, or victim awareness programmes had been run. Sometimes this involved bringing volunteers from the community into prisons who would share with prisoners the impact that crime had had on their lives.

While I was at the Partnership, individual Prison Officers tried to introduce 'Restorative Conferencing' (a type of RJ mediation) into the adjudication process, particularly at HMYOI Aylesbury and HMYOI Huntercombe, but it didn't work. It took too long to get everyone involved in an incident to agree to such a process, then set it up and fit it into the busy routine. Trying to introduce anything new into a prison regime anyway can make you feel like you are Canute trying to halt the tide.

This is not to say of course, that restorative practice does not happen routinely in prisons. Prison Officers everyday have to mediate between prisoners to try and keep the peace. And HMP Grendon, a prison which runs as a therapeutic community, was in our area. In therapeutic communities members are challenged about the effect of their behaviour on others, and where possible are expected to make amends.

I trained as an RJ facilitator and full of enthusiasm practised mediation on my kids who were now aged 5 and 8. After yet another fight, I made them sit down and tediously consider the impact of their behaviour on each other for what seemed like hours. At the end they swore that they would never do it again - it was such an awful experience. For weeks after that, I only had to whisper that I would be making them mediate and they would instantly stop attacking each other. This wasn't how mediation is supposed to work, but it was undoubtedly effective.

I learned that there were many, often hidden, areas of 'deprivation among affluence' within the Thames Valley. In contrast some of our supporter groups were extremely wealthy - a colleague of mine attended one very lavish fund-raising dinner being hosted for us, and received an invitation generously mentioning that his driver would also be accommodated on the night. I struggled a little emotionally with the blatant inequality of things like this. That mansion was a long way from the

Britwell estate. Not that any of us weren't grateful of course for the donations.

The local High Sheriffs championed our work, regularly raising money for us, and tended to represent some of our wealthier benefactors. The role of the High Sheriff nowadays is largely ceremonial. Unpaid, High Sheriffs are required to attend royal visits and look after High Court Judges when they are in the area. The selection of new High Sheriffs is made annually by the Sovereign by the historic custom of 'pricking' the appointee's name with a bodkin. Their uniform has remained essentially unchanged since the late seventeenth century and consists of a black or dark blue velvet coat with cut-steel buttons, breeches, shoes with cut-steel buckles, a sword, and a cocked hat. For obvious reasons, they did not wear this remarkable outfit when they went into secondary schools to give talks about their work. However good the discipline, young people only have so much self-control.

One of our High Sheriffs, William, was a kindly and very posh young man. I was due to accompany him on a visit to a Pupil Referral Unit. These schools hold children unable to remain in mainstream education. I arrived early, pressed the buzzer and after identifying myself was let in, before being escorted to the school secretary's office to wait. A little while later an excited small boy about the age of 11 was brought in, his teacher holding firmly onto his shoulders. After berating him for his misdemeanours she sat him down on a chair, ordered him not to move and left the office on some errand.

As soon as she had gone the intercom crackled into life. I heard the hesitant, cut-glass tones of the High Sheriff. The small boy listened for a few seconds then leapt up, marched across the room, picked up the intercom and with absolute determination and at the top of his lungs yelled: "FUCK OFF!" Poor William. I couldn't see him but I could visualise how high he jumped.

There was one other project which was particularly dear to my heart: the Partnership was very keen to support children and young people. In 1997 the mothers and fathers of more than 125,000 children were sent to prison. Very often, the fact that a child has a parent or sibling in prison is hidden from everyone around them, but the impact on them can be devastating. I was asked to write a leaflet for teachers explaining some ways in which they might be able to help if they become aware that a child is in this situation.

The leaflet *'Invisible Children'* wasn't much but it was something I could do. I wished and hoped I might be able to do more in the future.

Towards the end of my two years' secondment, the Prison Service finally realised that putting someone briefly in front of a three person board often did not always result in the right people being selected or promoted. This could be particularly disastrous for the appointment of Governing Governors. They therefore introduced, just for the selection of Governing Governors, the 'Suitable to be in Charge Assessment Centre'. This event involved a long barrage of tests and role-plays designed to avoid the risk of bias so common with the traditional board. I applied, attended the centre, and to my delight and relief was successful.

Finding somewhere to govern was not easy. I took some days out from the Partnership to visit prisons, applying for a couple of posts that were advertised. Touring round one windswept distant establishment I was greeted graciously at the door of his prefabricated cell by ex MP and peer of the realm Jeffrey Archer wearing a rather beautiful dressing gown. A gilded creature in a rusty cage. Once, I was told that I had been appointed to run a prison only to have the offer withdrawn a week later, as another Governor needed to be moved in fast from somewhere else: he had really, REALLY upset his Prison Officers Association.

There were weeks of uncertainty, and it was very stressful. We were more flexible now as both my parents had died and there was nothing tying us to the area. However, Daughter Number One was soon to transfer into secondary school, so if we were going to move, we needed to do it quickly. Frustrated that I could not control the situation, having read somewhere that a way of managing stress is to 'control what you can control', for the first time in my life I had my ears pierced. Within a fortnight, one was infected and scar tissue was already forming: I hoped this wasn't an omen for the future.

Then I got the call: "Brockhill needs a Governor", the voice began, "and I wondered..."

"Yes," I broke in."I'll do it!" The voice paused.

"Before you decide, let me tell you a little more...."

Chapter 11: Hope and Hell

HMP Brockhill, Worcestershire, 2002

The mother of a vulnerable woman who has taken her life in custody is now picketing every women's prison when someone dies. She arrives two days after we lose our first woman. Worried, I watch her out of the admin window for a while. Her placards shriek a warning to all, including incoming prisoners, that they can expect certain death inside. They are frightened enough as it is. I go out to try to reason with her. She is around 50 with rather wild grey hair, her face heavily lined. I invite her in to have a cup of tea and talk, but she avoids my eyes and shrugs me off. She doesn't leave for hours. I don't blame her. It's all that she can do. Maybe it's all that any of us can do.

HMP Brockhill, Worcestershire, 2002-2004

I was appointed Governor of Brockhill on 22 May 2002, aged 40. The prison was very small holding only 150 women, a hideous little 1960s build resembling a pile of embarrassed grey rubble, in the shadow of its brazen modern neighbour the monolithic HMP Blakenhurst. All the buildings were cramped and shabby. Not a great environment for anyone to live or work in.

We bought a rambling Victorian house on the outskirts of Redditch, about 7 miles from the gaol. I moved in first, camping in the attic on the floor in a sleeping bag, woken at some unearthly hour every morning by the next door neighbour's cockerel.

The house came with a massive garden complete with a bluebell wood and towering trees. The garden was far too large for us to maintain and it soon ran wild. We inherited with it a dilapidated open air swimming pool which was always freezing and already beginning to crack apart. We kept it going long enough for the kids to enjoy while they were still young, before nature reclaimed it. Sunlit, splashy days, which were to sustain me during the difficult months to come.

My operational management team included three governor grades and three Principal Officers. The team changed a few times but several people remain particularly etched in my mind.

My Deputy, Rowena, was formidable. She had been through some tough times and was raising a young son by herself. She had a laugh that could wake up a wing and she was a force to be reckoned with. She was a definite asset to have by one's side.

Hazel was there too, of course, who had once trained as a Prison Officer with me. Now she was a Governor Grade 5, quieter, very competent, still witty. It was good to see her again.

Narinder was another Governor 5. He was hard working and very deferential to me, reflecting the importance his Sikh faith placed on respecting authority. No one had ever paid me anything like so much respect before and it took a little getting used to.

I was to be grateful to a number of other people who were to support me. It was lovely and a shock to have a personal secretary for the first time, Grace, who would guard the door to my tiny office like a sweet, but no-nonsense dragon. She would manage the paperwork, organise my diary, and make me many, many necessary cups of tea.

I also grew to really appreciate the Chaplains. No Governor should contemplate running a prison without being able to call on a Chaplain they trust for when the worst happens. They can handle death when the rest of us flounder.

Holloway had not prepared me for managing such vulnerable women. The shock of being responsible for keeping this population alive hit me immediately like a shovel. The risk of suicide at Brockhill was terrifying and self-injury was endemic. The Service had introduced a new suicide and self-harm monitoring system. Prisoners at risk would be subject to either a constant watch, or hourly, 30 minute or 15 minute checks. It wasn't unusual for a third of the gaol to be on the list.

We were only aware of the most serious acts of self-injury, and these were an everyday occurrence. Many of our women self-injured constantly, not caring if they lived or died, such was their distress, hopelessness or anger. The methods some used could prove lethal if they weren't interrupted, or if they made a mistake.

And there were always a few who had determinedly given up on living.

I was soon dreading the first death.

After the first, I went home very late, white with fatigue. I had phoned my husband and told him what had happened. A hug of worried children bearing flowers met me at the door.

I was on the scene when we tried and failed to revive another woman. I stood there, the cell door digging into my back, offering feeble words of encouragement to the staff as they fought to resuscitate her until the ambulance crew eventually arrived. It felt like hours. Even when you know in your heart of hearts it's no good, you keep going. Both because it's protocol unless the body is in rigour, but also for the prisoner's family, so that they would know that we had done everything we could, and not given up.

Dana, only 18, took her life on the Young Offender wing and the prison reeled with shock and grief. Attending the little memorial service I watched prisoners and staff openly crying. I cried too.

Then Lisa took her life on the 'enhanced' wing. This wing was where the most trusted, settled prisoners were located and she had earned her place. No one expects someone to kill themselves on the enhanced wing. A prison Listener[12] had talked with her in the days beforehand. The Samaritans[13], who ran the Listeners scheme, gave the Listener and us much support in the dark days following.

---

[12] The Listener scheme aims to reduce suicide and self-harm in prisons. Samaritans select, train and support prisoners to become volunteer Listeners, and they provide confidential emotional support to their peers. The first Listener scheme was introduced at HMP Swansea in 1991, and is still going strong today.

[13] www.samaritans.org

I was informed of one death when we were on an adventure holiday on Dartmoor, in our old camper van. There was little point in returning straight away. The van only went about 40mph, it would have taken hours to get back, and there was little in practice I could have done that people weren't already doing. It would also have ruined the children's holiday. But I felt terribly guilty not being there. After that, when we took a family holiday, we left the country.

'Near misses'- where prisoners tried to kill themselves but were saved in the nick of time - were frequent and also terrifying.

I remember patting a shaken member of staff on the shoulder as he sat in the wing office, saying to him, inadequately, but honestly: "You've saved another life today, Roy." It was an amazing, and horrible, achievement. And one he did not want.

I always went into the prison on Christmas Day. In the space of an hour and a half we experienced two near misses. I discovered a member of staff sitting on a landing floor crying with shock.

Senior Officer Tyler on duty in the segregation unit, intervened and saved a woman moments before it was too late. It was one time too many. He ran straight out of the gaol, yelling as he did so that he had had enough and was resigning. He was persuaded back after a few weeks but soon left again, eventually emigrating to New Zealand.

Juliet, an Officer in her thirties, went 'long-term sick'. I visited her at home and she told me that she was unable to physically lock a door on a prisoner anymore. Every time she had gone off duty she had been making a young woman, before she had locked her in, promise that she would not hurt herself. But then the girl had done so, and nearly died.

Nearly all our reportable 'incidents' when they occurred, involved women trying to harm themselves. These are the statistics for recorded incidents, for one year during my time at Brockhill, compiled by the ombudsman. Shocking figures for such a tiny prison:

670	incidents of self-harm
114	prisoners attempted self-harm
47	prisoners required resuscitation at the scene
14	prisoners required outside hospital treatment
243	incidents of attempted self strangulation
211	incidents of women cutting themselves
68	attempted hangings
26	instances in which prisoners aggravated existing wounds
14	occasions of prisoners burning themselves
14	instances of attempted self suffocation
35	incidents of injury through head butting/wall punching
505	F2052SHs (at risk forms) were opened, of which 441 were closed
29	occasions the crisis suite was used
46	constant watches
1	death

I often felt personally helpless. I recall talking with one young woman, Amy, through the open hatch in her door, trying to reason with her. She was young and small with wizened features and she grinned at me in malicious delight as she slowly and methodically removed with her fingers each of the stitches on her scarred arm. In that moment, Amy was directing her rage at me by continuing to self-injure, and there was absolutely nothing I could do about it.

After each fatality we were rightfully criticised if in any way we failed to follow our own procedures or best practice, or if we didn't take notice of, or failed to pick up, information shared with us by other agencies. Individual staff also had to be prepared to face hearing their best judgements scrutinised in the Coroner's court before bereaved families. Staff were really good at recognising and responding to distress, but some women intent on harming themselves were expert in concealing their intentions. We could not rely on what they would tell us, and that was very hard for people to come to terms with.

I had to give evidence at inquests at the Coroner's Court in Stourbridge concerning the deaths of prisoners who had died prior to my arrival. One of these had occurred more than three years previously. Nothing prepares you for this, or for what to say to the family of the prisoner when you encounter them - if they want to meet your eyes.

More than a year after I left the prison, I was to attend and give evidence at inquests for the prisoners who had died under my watch. I only have a few memories of those days: Being desperate to ensure a truth is really understood. Exchanging a glance. Attempting to offer a condolence. Waiting for hours in bleak rooms, drinking tea from paper cups. Overwhelming sadness.

Shortly after I arrived at Brockhill I attended a joint NHS consultative committee meeting in the town.

When asked to report what I was dealing with I did not hold back. I was quietly boiling with anger. If I had noticed that the press was there it did not register, or maybe it did and I didn't care. The headline in the Worcester News a few days afterwards read:

'Amazed' not a death every day!
The Governor of Brockhill women's prison near Redditch says she is 'amazed' there is not a death in her prison every day.

I rang the Prison Service Press Office to confess what I had done. I told them how high the risk was of our vulnerable women dying and what little we could do to keep them safe.

"That's not something we say," they spluttered.

"I'm afraid I did say it," I said, "because it's true."

"But we don't say it." They repeated.

I promised I would not say it again. At least not like that.

Many of our women were traumatised prior to coming into prison through sexual abuse or domestic violence. Many unsurprisingly had mental health problems in addition. I was mindful that we risked revictimising them through the prison processes. I became particularly concerned, as many others already were, by the psychological effect on women of the 'full' search (usually called the 'strip' search) which women had to undergo routinely whenever they entered prison or left under escort, or if it was suspected that they had concealed an illicit item. I was also concerned about the effects on the women when we needed to restrain them because of their behaviour, or an act of self-injury. Then triggered by memories of abuse they might panic, or, if gripped by some nightmare delusion, they might feel they needed to fight for their lives. Everyone could get badly injured.

Some of the women were so vulnerable that things others said, or did, would trigger distress and self-injury. I upset the pagan minister by confiscating a set of tarot cards from one woman. We had so many disturbed and vulnerable women in the gaol that I did not want the cards getting into general circulation, and I didn't trust a particular prisoner to keep her cards to herself.

Anniversaries of personal loss, and national holidays, were particularly sensitive times. Mother's Day church services were poorly attended: deemed too painful for some of the regular attendees. Christmas was not a time to celebrate.

Keeping the prison regime going was very difficult. If two serious incidents occurred, such as the hospitalisation of a prisoner and a prisoner needing a constant watch, it could be disastrous. Moreover, locking the prison down to produce the necessary staff to respond to such events had serious consequences. Women confined to their cells would be more likely to self-injury. At night it was even worse, there were less staff on duty, so sometimes staff had to be ordered from their beds into the prison. I even ended up on a couple of occasions, rushing out to temporarily staff bedwatches myself, which would have been unheard of elsewhere for a Governor. It was always a shock when we occasionally managed to take staff away from the rota to undertake necessary refresher training. As a management team we reviewed daily, every member of staff reporting sick, doing all we could to support them. I rarely, if ever, suspected anyone was not genuinely ill.

I was constantly aware of how vulnerable our staffing situation was and our ability to respond to emergencies. Even when I was at home, I was on alert.

I used to dread the phone ringing at night.

Some of the women were very difficult to comprehend. A young woman was forever provoking staff to physically move her. She was not violent and did not seem particularly distressed, she just would not budge sometimes when we really needed her to. I began to suspect she just wanted to be held.

In the middle of the night I was rung by Fiona, the Night Orderly Officer. She had spent two hours listening to a prisoner who had rung her bell, asked to speak to her, and then confessed to multiple murders committed alongside her partner. She gave horrific, detailed accounts of the crimes, complete with descriptions of where bodies were buried. Fiona believed what she was saying and was very shaken. I came into the prison to debrief her. I usually carried chocolate during night visits to share with staff and I administered a fair bit that night.

Neither Fiona, nor the prisoner, were interviewed by the police to my knowledge. I can only assume that the woman was known to fantasise.

Some prisoners were exceptionally challenging to manage. The father of a woman died and she requested to go to the funeral. Maisie was a habitual crack user, which we were sure had affected her brain, as her behaviour was very unpredictable and extremely aggressive. She was also of mighty proportions and looked like she could flatten a tank. I was immediately lobbied by several members of her close family pleading for us not to let her go, terrified of how she would behave.

After further discussion with the family, it was agreed she ought to attend, but the question of how to manage it remained. My Deputy Rowena came to my rescue. She knew the prisoner well. "I'll take her", she said. "She won't mess with me".

They went. Maisie remained handcuffed to Rowena throughout, and behaved impeccably. They both sang the hymns with all their might. The service, I was told, was beautiful.

Every day had new challenges. A prisoner's mother rang us to say that her 23 year old adult daughter, Marybelle, in our custody, was actually only 13 years old. They were travellers and she claimed that the girl had swapped identities with her cousin. This seriously worried us: we were potentially holding a young child in custody, and among adult prisoners to boot! Despite the mother taking her daughter's birth certificate to the police station, they failed to believe her. The daughter, a cheerful young person who seemed perfectly happy with her situation, agreed with her mother but said she "wasn't bothered" where she was held. Advice from the Prison Service was that we could only hold her in conditions determined by her warrant. No one appeared to have the means, at least in the short-term, to prove her age. At that point we had a wing which held at one end juveniles (ages 15-17) and the other end young offenders (18-21). I decided to ignore all the advice and put her there, in the middle of the wing, in a single cell. That removed her from the adult wing at least, while everyone continued to argue. Luckily not long afterwards, she was bailed.

For some prisoners, tragically, this was their home and they were anything but 'gate happy' when the time came for them to leave. They counted the staff as their friends and family and they felt safe - far safer than in the scary outside world. Here they had food, shelter, clothing and we could help them with their drug issues. I arrived one morning to discover a woman, Mollie, lying down in front of the gate, sobbing and refusing to move. Another had to be coaxed into a taxi and accompanied by her favourite member of staff all the way to her hometown where she was prised out of the taxi and into the care of her Probation Officer. Other women arrived back with us quickly and relieved, having committed some hopefully minor offence.

Not all were glad to be in prison, of course. Some were furious. And a very few were dangerous - the arsonists particularly. Staff would risk their lives going into cells to rescue prisoners: at that time no smoke hoods were available. After one such occasion Officer Bailey emerged reeking of smoke, red-eyed. "I need a fag", he panted. "Anyone got a light?" An excellent member of staff, Mr Bailey was the prison clown, and always good for lightening the tension.

I had spent 18 years working in male prisons. I was learning a lot about women prisoners, particularly how they behaved differently.

Women didn't seem that interested in 'concerted indiscipline'. We had a couple of food fights, more to break the routine than anything. Bread rolls on the menu were a mistake. They made excellent missiles. One lunchtime however, I was informed a 'sit down protest' was underway. I made my way to what we euphemistically called the 'Control Room'. It was actually an office where a couple of Officer Support Grades operated the radio net.

Already in there was Larry, a very experienced Principal Officer who had previously worked at a large male prison nearby. He was the strong silent type. He would patiently wait for everyone else to stop gabbling, a slight smile on his weather-beaten face, before gently sharing the benefit of his wisdom.

It was policy to report to HQ as soon as any act of concerted indiscipline had lasted over fifteen minutes. HQ would then begin to set up a London command centre and appoint a 'Gold' Commander. Fifteen minutes had passed and I reached for the phone, but Larry touched my arm. "Wait." He said. "Not yet. The women will have a bit of a chat about this and that, then they'll get up and wander back to their rooms. It'll take about another ten minutes." He was dependable, and he was right.

The women did like a bit of excitement. I was convinced the fire alarms were being regularly set off simply because they enjoyed the sight of fit firefighters coming to their rescue. Eventually we agreed with the fire service that they would park their vehicles at the gate while our own staff checked the 'fire' out, to deter the miscreants from wasting their time and save their colleagues from the raucous cat calls.

As a consequence of what we were dealing with, on many days the prison was a sea of whirling emotions. You had to ride the waves, or go under.

It was not a place where one could rely on reason and logic alone to operate.

I asked Larry if he actually enjoyed working in this maelstrom: it was such a contrast to his previous establishment. He grinned at me. "It's great", he said. "No one's trying to kill me here".

The positive side of an environment where there was so much distress and vulnerability was that the women were very supportive and usually amazingly tolerant towards each other. I received a phone call warning me that a well known prisoner who had been involved in the notorious murder of a child, would be lodging at the prison for a few days. It was agreed however, that she would not need segregation. This would have been inconceivable in the male estate.

Prisoners supported us too. It was not unusual to see a woman put an arm around a member of staff after a bad incident and it was common for them to ask us how we were.

Juliet, who had finally decided to request a transfer, came to say goodbye. She said: "I've loved working here. Everyone's so caring....it's just the self-harm I can't deal with".

To relieve the stress we lived for the odd funny moment. A large goose crash-landed in the prison and seemed unable to take off again. It wandered around the exercise yard for hours watched by fascinated spectators. It was not until the RSPCA were on the road that it remembered its flightpath out.

The rabbits too provided us with little daily diversions. One young woman Cerys, who had learning difficulties, used to regularly run off from staff escorting her around the prison. They would pursue her at their leisure. They knew where she would be: up the hill, round the back of the prison, chasing the rabbits and having a ball.

The rabbits used to expire though with sad regularity. One somehow ended up deceased right in the middle of the prison pond which was difficult enough to deal with, but the bunny we had the most trouble extracting expired right under the very middle of the Court Video Links portacabin.[14]

One of the last actions my predecessor had taken before their departure was to suspend the Chair of the POA, a powerful person within the establishment, following a number of allegations. Industrial relations at the gaol when I arrived were, understandably, very sensitive. Eventually investigation into these allegations concluded and the Chair was charged under the Prison Service staff disciplinary code. My boss decided that a Governor independent of the prison ought to conduct the hearing. I didn't argue. It might make my job easier trying to bring the prison back together again afterwards, whatever the outcome. The member of staff was found guilty of two charges: firstly of using offensive behaviour and language to colleagues and secondly of failure to obey an order, and was dismissed from the

---

[14] In certain court proceedings such as bail hearings prisoners may be allowed to appear in court via video-link rather than attend in person.

Service. This caused a shockwave and some division throughout the prison.

Months later she appealed to the Civil Service Appeal Board which I attended in London together with the adjudicating Governor. The CSAB upheld the finding but to our shock found the award had been too harsh concluding the applicant should not have been dismissed. Rather than reinstate her however, the Prison Service eventually chose to pay her compensation. I was relieved the matter was concluded and the prison settled down again.

I soon had other serious staff issues to deal with.

I received a summons to appear in front of an Industrial Tribunal after a nurse, Ms Pence, accused me of something. I can't even remember what it was now, but I do remember I felt the issue was patently ridiculous. I sought advice from the Treasury Solicitor, as was the usual practice, and spent hours preparing a defence. Myself and the Treasury Solicitor duly appeared at the IT together with Pence and Richard, the new Chair of our local

Prison Officers' Association who was representing her.

On the day the Industrial Tribunal gave the case short shrift. We were awarded costs but I chose not to ask for damages. The morning afterwards, Richard arrived in my office. He began by saying he thought it was 'bad form' that I had availed myself of professional advice(!) and said on that basis, he thought it would be only fair if I would let Pence off paying the costs. Livid and restraining myself from suggesting that the advice the POA had given her couldn't have been that great, I told him exactly what I thought of all the work his client had given me and declined the request.

I had to sack my first member of staff at Brockhill. Mr Blake, a probationary Prison Officer, had a habit of creeping up on the women Officer Support Grades and kissing them on the back of their necks. He claimed he was merely being friendly as he was with everyone, but looked horrified when I asked casually if he kissed his male friends on the back of their necks too. Maybe he had slept through the sexual harassment lecture at the Officers Training School. I hated sacking him but he was too much of a risk to keep.

When I first arrived at Brockhill I was briefed that there was a long-standing issue with an alcoholic Officer. For years Charlie had been regularly discovered 'under the influence' and given multiple chances and offers of help. He was well liked and often protected by staff, although they would admit when pushed, that he was something of a liability. I was informed on the quiet, that the Director General had visited the prison once, and was completely unaware that, when he had been issued his keys, Charlie had been dead drunk and asleep under the counter.

A report about Charlie came to me a few months after my arrival. This time it had emanated from a prisoner. Charlie was on duty, and his breath was smelling of alcohol. I summoned him to my office. He reeked of cheese and onion crisps, which I suspected he had hurriedly eaten to try to mask the smell (which they didn't) and I told him so.

I offered him support, pointed him to sources of help, and told him that this had to stop. He thanked me and promised me faithfully that it would. I also requested him to lay off eating cheese and onion crisps at work "*for the avoidance of doubt*".

Several months later I was told Charlie was again in the prison having been drinking. I summoned him to my office and smelt alcohol on his breath. I called in a witness who confirmed my observation and I suspended Charlie from duty. I reported to my boss what had happened, another Governor was dispatched to investigate (as I was a witness) and a disciplinary hearing followed. This Governor gave Charlie an official warning and transferred him to a neighbouring prison. The same thing happened again in the new prison and yet another disciplinary hearing ensued. Finally he was dismissed. Charlie had originally been a good

Officer and was a loss to the Service. Addiction is a terrible thing.

Late one afternoon I received a report that a male Officer might be having an inappropriate relationship with a prisoner: the evidence being that he had been seen with his shirt partly undone coming out of her room. I am personally, greatly in favour of male staff working in women's prisons - they can be positive role models of caring men - often the few decent men the women have ever encountered. I was prepared to give him the benefit of the doubt.

I interviewed Officer Steve Wyatt. He smiled sadly at me. According to him, it was all lies. The woman was messing about and threw some water at him as a joke and he had rung out his shirt. Wyatt was in his late thirties, well-built and filled the chair. Word was that he oiled his muscles. Wyatt I was also informed, had a secret sideline. He was a part-time stuntman in films and TV.

The woman, Gail, was in her late twenties, a recovering addict and doing her best to stay clean. She had the usual troubled background including abuse. She was blonde and attractive and obviously made an effort over her appearance. She appeared very worried and defensive.

We detailed Wyatt to a different wing so that he and the prisoner could not come into easy contact. The rumours went quiet and Gail was later released.

Some weeks went by. Then a member of staff told me they had seen the two of them, standing together by the side of a road in a nearby town. When I challenged him, Wyatt claimed it was a coincidence: they had met, he had said hello, then he had walked on.

Several weeks later, Richard, POA Chair, arrived in my office. He informed me that a week before, he had encountered Wyatt and ex-prisoner Gail in his local Budgens supermarket. Wyatt, he said, admitted that he had been meeting her. He claimed that he had encountered her again when their eyes met romantically over the strawberries counter; they had, allegedly, *"fallen for each other"*, meeting up several times since (mostly in Budgens coffee shop!) and they were now, he said, *"in a relationship"*. Wyatt had added with a wink that Gail was *"a real looker"* and he trusted Richard not to tell anyone. I thanked Richard for the information, adding a tad sarcastically that it was a shame that it had taken him a week to decide to tell me. I called Wyatt in. He denied everything and promptly went off sick with 'stress'.

To add insult to injury I was then informed that Wyatt was still touting for work as a stuntman while I was paying him to be sick.

I discussed the situation with a Governor colleague. "You can hire a private detective, you know", he said.

"I can do that?" I asked incredulously, visions of Hercule Poirot in my head.

The private detective wasn't very much like Poirot. He was casually dressed, red faced and full of zeal. He shook my hand vigorously. "Call me 'Al'", he said.

I asked him if he could search for any evidence that Wyatt was seeing the ex-prisoner and find out whether he was genuinely sick. Al reported a fortnight later. He announced he couldn't prove the relationship but did have news on the alleged 'moonlighting'.

He had phoned Wyatt claiming to be a casting agent looking for stunt men for an important, unspecified film, shortly to start shooting in London. He had explained to him that he had to be mysterious about the details, because of the "*high profile nature of the project*". The new Harry Potter was about to start filming and it was obvious that that was what Al was describing. Wyatt bought it. He gave Al his complete availability for work with immediate effect. I immediately wrote to Wyatt telling him I had good reason to believe that he was not genuinely sick and I was stopping his pay. He returned to work two days later.

To our surprise, Gail the prisoner, then suddenly appeared back too, having committed some minor offence. Now I had them both back in the gaol. But that was nothing compared to the shock of what was to follow: the news swept the prison like wildfire - she was pregnant! I briefly wondered if anyone had ever produced a DNA test to prove paternity at a staff disciplinary hearing, but decided that this was veering into the realms of fantasy. Instead we began listening very carefully to all her telephone calls. All calls to and from prisoners, except with their legal advisers, are recorded. It was crystal clear that she and Wyatt were phoning each other. They were very bad at deception. They used aliases for each other but kept forgetting them. And we recognised their voices.

I informed Wyatt that I was charging him with 'Bringing the Service into Disrepute' and suspended him. He knew the game was up and resigned.

We transferred Gail to a prison more able to meet her needs and those of her baby. We took no disciplinary action against her. Her only mistake was falling for this man. She was vulnerable. He was a predator.

Corrupt staff of course were a tiny minority. The majority of staff at Brockhill were doing battle everyday to care for their charges and keep them alive. And while they were under such pressure they had to endure screaming headlines in the media about what was happening in women's prisons. For some people the Prison Officer's uniform would always symbolise brutality, control and oppression.

Staff at Brockhill had access to a confidential telephone support line and their peer support Care Team, but I wanted to offer something more. By shifting some money around we managed to employ an onsite counsellor. Mr Polly was a gentle little man who would wander the prison, quietly getting to know the staff. They began to unload on him things they were wary of their peers as well as their managers knowing. I gave Mr Polly a badge saying 'Staff Counsellor'. I thought it important that the staff saw unequivocally that he was 'for them'.

I would quite often receive letters and cards from prisoners after they had left, thanking us for the help they had been given. Reading them always made me feel encouraged. We put up a large display board in the gatelodge, erased all the personal details on the letters and cards and stuck them up. The staff used to muster in the gatelodge while the final wing roll calls were being completed, and they would read them. I wanted them to be reminded how much they had made a difference to these women's lives. They were also read by visitors to the prison, some of whom arrived with only negative preconceived views.

At Christmas I wanted to do something to thank the staff for their efforts. Some who had worked at the nearby private prison spoke wistfully about how every year they had each been given a Christmas turkey. Something like that was out of the question in the public sector. I decided the least I could do was to handwrite every member of staff a personal Christmas card. Many days, and several doses of ibuprofen later, this had proved to be a really silly idea. I did not repeat it.

I decided to offer a hard incentive to staff who had managed a whole year's attendance without taking a single day off sick for any reason. After a huge amount of argument about what might be acceptable, we awarded these heroes a compact disc player. The next year, I became even more ambitious and negotiated a deal for a spa day voucher. To my intense annoyance, by the time the end of the year came the spa refused to honour the deal. I wouldn't pay what they wanted, went elsewhere, and ended up paying more. I was slightly put out when one of the recipients gave her award away, apparently deciding it was "*nice but a bit weird*". Spa days had not yet become fashionable.

I knew the importance of clear and frequent communication and I began sending out news bulletins through the new computer network but was initially disappointed that few people seemed to be reading them. I wondered if they were still struggling with the new technology. That was until I announced we were considering demolishing the staff bike shed. I was deluged with indignant replies. They read that all right.

I was forced to improve my public speaking, something I did not enjoy, sometimes having to address quite intimidating staff meetings. Luckily my acting instincts would kick in and allow me to appear rather more confident than I felt. I even fancied I had unconsciously channelled a passable Henry V, after doing my best to rally the troops during one crisis.

We began to make improvements to the women's regime. Small in the national scheme of things but significant to the prison.

As a local gaol, most of our prisoners did not stay very long so it was unrealistic to run lengthy skills training. Our regime consisted of short education schemes, mainly literacy, IT and maths and we introduced short catering and gardening courses.

A voluntary group brought in a trained 'pat dog' - a gentle Labrador - for some of the most vulnerable women to meet and love. We purchased some giant games, like Connect 4, for the women to play on the dismal asphalt exercise yards. We also developed a rolling drug awareness programme, decorating part of a storeroom to make it a little cosier as a venue, with sofas, a carpet and colourful cushions.

A major change came about nationally while I was at Brockhill which significantly benefited our drug addicts. Methadone maintenance programmes were introduced. Women usually began taking drugs to deaden the abuse they suffered and then became addicted. In prison withdrawal without support puts the risk of self-injury by women through the roof. When released women would often, immediately, take drugs again, frequently at higher strength, risking overdose and death. By offering methadone maintenance in the prison they could be stabilised, transition to the community safely, and in time, if they wished, gradually reduce their reliance on the medication. It didn't always work as smoothly as that and the practice was not without controversy, but to those of us who had seen desperate women in withdrawal, in pain and 'clucking' (shaking uncontrollably), this new regime was a godsend.

This was only available for heroin addicts though. There was nothing to offer those who took crack cocaine other than pain relief. And plenty of our women were alcoholics. Their withdrawal was extremely dangerous and had to be medically managed. Many women took combinations of these and other drugs and a few were so desperate that they would take anything they could get their hands on, buying or stealing other prisoners' medication.

When bullying incidents occurred it was nearly always over drugs. The most dreadful were serious sexual assaults commonly known as 'de-crutching', where a woman was attacked after being suspected by her peers of concealing drugs in her vagina.

The need to better support women who were at highest risk of death continued to keep me awake at nights. Julia Rose, a Counselling Psychologist, joined us from the University of Wolverhampton and developed a 'roll-on roll-off' programme we called 'Carousel', to support some of our most vulnerable women at risk of serious self-injury. This included physical exercise, coping skills, art and music.

Women would often disclose to us the terrible things they had suffered and occasionally, with support, they were brave enough to give evidence against their abusers to the police.

Not all of those who suffered in this way were prisoners. I once had a Prison Officer work for me who was in an abusive relationship. There may, of course, have been others unknown to me. Everyone knew that there were certain shifts, particularly around holidays, that Shelley could not be required to work or she would suffer the consequences. The situation had existed for years. She was referred to specialist support, but she felt completely trapped. I was worried that by going along with her partner's demands we were facilitating them and increasing his power over her. But we had to keep her safe.

As soon as I entered Brockhill I wanted to improve the visiting experience. Women prisoners get far fewer visitors than their male equivalents. Queues of women and children used to faithfully turn up each week to visit Blakenhurst - you could see them lining up at the Visitors Centre opposite. Often, I was sure, pressure was being put on them by the men. It was an expense many visitors didn't need, and not a lot of fun for small kids, even if they were glad to see their fathers, which sadly wasn't always the case. There was only ever a trickle of visitors queuing to get into Brockhill.

When a man with a family enters prison, his partner usually struggles on without him, looking after the kids and attempting to keep things together. When a woman goes into prison, even if she was with a partner beforehand, the kids usually end up living with extended family, or go into the Care system. Only very occasionally a relative would bring a child into Brockhill for a visit.

The saddest visits of all would be when a social worker would bring a child for a final visit to say goodbye, before their adoption. These visits would usually take place in the chapel.

We painted the stairways on the way up to the visits room with child-height cartoons and obtained some funding to create a small play area complete with toys. We managed to get this featured as a good news story for once, in the local newspaper. I roped in Daughter Number Two for a photo opportunity. She pretended to be a prisoner's child playing with the toys, one of her first acting challenges which she carried off with aplomb. She also temporarily solved another problem I'd been having. Gate staff were forever leaving the door to the gate lodge wide open. When I entered the prison with my excited little minion, she shot straight into the gate lodge and started trying to play with the keys. The door remained tightly shut after that for quite some time.

One battle I lost. The bus service down to the prison and its two neighbouring establishments was cut. Now families with elderly relatives and small children had to traipse down the long drive from the main road in all weathers, or pay for an expensive taxi from the railway station. I lobbied those that had the power to change the decision, but I got nowhere.

We tried to smarten up the place a little. We continually painted the corridors, and stuck up pictures of nature and seascapes. But the infrastructure was fast falling apart.

When I arrived most of the cell windows were corroded and would not close properly - women would try to block the draughts with sanitary towels. Eventually the argument to replace them was won and gradually work began.

In an effort to make their rooms seem a little more homely, I ordered a beautiful pair of curtains for each. They were the colours of the tropics - greens and yellows and blues. I hadn't allowed for the vagaries of Prison Industries: they sent us 400 left-fitting curtains.

Brockhill was one of the few prisons in the country with an automatic sanitation system. It was designed to let only one prisoner out of her room at a time to use the toilet. Even then it broke down regularly, and although the Officer Support Grades in the Control Room had the power to override the system, women could be waiting a long time to be let out of their cells.

Sometimes the women would misuse the system to their own advantage, to push roll-ups under the doors of friends or have a brief chat. But even so this was not an appropriate system for women. Many would be menstruating and some were pregnant: all needed immediate access to a toilet.

I researched how much it would cost to install integral sanitation but was told in no uncertain terms that it was uneconomical to pour more money into such a small prison.

Next the kitchen was deemed unfit for purpose, although not before a heavy box of chocolate eclairs had fallen out of a high cupboard and nearly seen off one of the caterers. For months food had to be cooked by the open prison up the road and towed down the hill in a series of trolleys chained together like one of the little trains you see in holiday camps. It was amazing that meals were usually still hot when they were served.

In the continued total absence of a health care centre, we had no choice but to hold severely disturbed and ill prisoners whose presence on the wings could not be sustained, in the tiny three celled grim segregation unit. For a week a woman conducted a 'dirty protest'[15] in one and staff had to manage this. It was abhorrent to expect us to hold

---

[15] Where a prisoner spreads faeces and urine around their cell.

mentally ill women in such a place. I walked in on a woman in her forties located there, whom someone had decided should be given a phone to call her young child. She was screaming down the phone in rage, beads of sweat running down her forehead: *"Get me out of here!"* and *"It's all your fault!"* In an instance, I was the child on the end of the phone, small and powerless, watching the rain drip down the window, hoping my father would return from work.

By the end of 2003 however, progress was finally being made in the construction of our brand new healthcare centre. It was to be a grand day when I was eventually asked to choose the colour of the carpet.

As well as pursuing the improvements we wanted to make and fire-fighting incidents each day, we had to obey the demands of our masters. These included passing a variety of audits and preparing for visits from Her Majesty's Inspector of Prisons. The latter could also occur without warning. Both the audit system and the Inspectorate exist for good reason but both involve weeks, sometimes months of work. A bad report can have scarring results for the establishment and everyone involved. We had to demonstrate that we were on the way up.

Security had not been the highest priority at Brockhill and the written systems were a mess. Hazel took on the task and did a stirling job but I was not optimistic - it had been so long neglected. Staff panicked on the morning of the audit. From somewhere arose the idea that it was not acceptable to have cutlery simply lying around in drawers in the staff kitchen in the admin block. It should, someone suggested, be carefully displayed on a shadow board, like it was in the wing offices. As the inspectors marched in through the gate, staff stripped the cutlery from all the drawers and dumped the lot in my desk - the one place they imagined no one would search. Amazingly, somehow, we scraped through the audit.

One of our most irritating successes with HM Inspectorate came out of a recommendation from their last report. For some unknown reason the long drive from the main road down to the prisons had been constructed with the highest speed bumps known to mankind and had written off one of the Inspectors' fuel tanks. It took significant cost, time and effort by the neighbouring male prisoner workforce to cut the bumps down to size. When the Inspectorate returned, they didn't notice any difference.

Despite the challenges, nearly two years in post, I was now relishing being in charge. I had the opportunity to make my own decisions, experiment a little, and be creative. Plans made, surprisingly, often worked. Staff returned from long term sick. Sometimes we went a week without a serious incident. On the days when nothing awful had happened I went home feeling really satisfied.

We were having some success. I was informed by a senior manager that 'word was' Brockhill: "*wasn't quite as bad as it had been!*"

Then Press Office rang.

The Prison Service has generally had a 'hate hate' relationship with the media.

Many people had been burnt. I had once witnessed a colleague turn white the day after he had enjoyed a liquid lunch in the pub with a journalist friend from the Brighton and Hove Argus and told all 'off the record'. The headlines the next day reported exactly what he had said about the Home Secretary.

And since I had been at Brockhill there had been a succession of red lurid headlines in the Birmingham Mail about every nasty issue we were dealing with. I was positive we had at least one mole on staff. I had announced as much in a notice to staff and told them how despicable I thought this was - particularly as I assumed the person was being paid. It seemed to work - the stories stopped.

To be fair it probably didn't help that the Prison Service had usually refused to let any press or media into gaols. There had never been any modern, positive stories told, least of all about women's prisons.

Now however, for the first time, it seemed that the Press Office was trying to build bridges with the media and wanted me to cooperate. But I wasn't optimistic.

A Guardian journalist arrived. The women were excited as always by a stranger in their midst and the youngsters played up, multiple scuffles breaking out all over the establishment. No one was hurt however, and by the end of the day our visitor had learned the skill of slamming himself backwards against the corridor wall when the alarm sounded, to allow maximum space for the stampeding staff to pass by.

The headline when published was not great:

"Women burn, strangle and stab themselves in jail hell"

Despite this, the author voiced sympathy for what we were trying to do, particularly given the conditions we were forced to operate in.

A BBC news crew arrived next. This was to annoy me on two accounts. I didn't fancy being on camera much, particularly in what I was suddenly convinced was a decidedly unflattering suit. All that chocolate hadn't done me any favours. Jokingly, I mentioned this and the pleasant journo, who I imagined I had developed a rapport with, promised to film me from the waist up. She lied. Secondly, the first statement she hit me with when the cameras started rolling was my infamous quote from the healthcare meeting about how I was *"amazed there is not a death every day"*. As I responded, I gave her a look that could have killed her.

We attracted a lot of local press attention too. BBC Radio Hereford and Worcester lined up a live debate between myself and the chair of the Prison Reform Trust expecting a fight, but we basically agreed with each other over the vulnerability of women in prison and how most of them should be managed in the community, if only someone would find the resources and the will to make it happen. I think the journalist was disappointed.

Then, I was informed a VIP was on the way.

Cherie Blair arrived in a white suit and high heels, a brave choice I thought for a visit to a prison. I hoped the young offenders we were due to meet in the education department weren't engaged in anything too messy. Luckily we didn't have any iron stairs to climb - always fatal for anyone wearing heels. They get stuck in the holes. For security reasons I had not told anyone the identity of our guest and only a few knew we were expecting a visitor at all. The prisoners were thrilled to find someone they recognised from the TV in their company and the place became manic as the news spread. Mrs Blair, a lawyer, handled the random questions the women threw at her (including those about her sex life with her husband) with ease. I made rather more awkward conversation with her about the idiosyncrasies of running a prison, and the delights of eBay. I thought it was a reasonably successful event.

Things were going relatively well (for Brockhill) at this stage, but unknown to me my time was running out.

When I took over Brockhill the 'Women's Estate' had just been created, and for the first time women's prisons were being managed separately from male prisons. The aim had been to ensure operational cooperation between women's prisons and a clear top-down focus on women's needs.

When I originally met him I thought my boss Andrew, the Head of the Women's Estate, rather resembled a villain from the silent movie era: the moustached kind that ties the heroine to a railway line. Despite his appearance however, he was tremendously enthusiastic about getting the best for our population and he really supported his Governors in their struggles. There had been a smaller Women's Policy team in London prior to this time, but he built on this creating an additional operational team based in Burton on Trent. Governors of Women's Prisons met there together regularly. I found sharing with colleagues really helpful especially as this was my first in-charge post. Andrew gave me good advice, was encouraging and trusted my judgement.

One day, in Spring 2004, when I had governed Brockhill for just over two years, things changed. We had been summoned to Burton upon Trent but not told the reason why. When I arrived you could cut the atmosphere with a knife. We took our places round the large table sensing something serious was about to happen. Andrew entered looking grim and sat down, his silent team surrounding him. "It's been decided that the Women's Estate is no more". He said bluntly. "All women's prisons are going to be managed by local Area Managers again".

"Why?" We gasped.

"It's a quick way to save the Service a lot of money". Andrew paused. "And for those of you who get **** (he named a particular Area Manager) "may God have mercy on your soul!"

He was talking to me.

Nothing really changed for a while at Brockhill. I began to feel a little more distanced from the other women's prisons and it wasn't quite so easy to do business, but I did enjoy getting to know the Governors of the local male prisons. The problems they were dealing with though, were very different from mine. Their focus was almost entirely on security. My presence did manage to embarrass the Governor of Blakenhurst however, when on a tour of his establishment we walked into his works department and discovered a spectacular display of pornography adorning the walls. It's amazing what you find when you go 'walkabout' in prisons and unlock doors no one is expecting you to.

Then my life became significantly more difficult.

The Area Manager I had been warned about who had inherited Brockhill, and yours truly working for him, seemed to me a very strange man. He appeared cold, detached and completely devoid of humour - he seemed to have a machine-like lack of human connection. 'Machine-like' isn't an entirely accurate description though: it implies he was without emotion. At our first meeting I felt he took an instant dislike to me. In the weeks to come, as he interrogated me curtly during his visits, I found him quite hostile, borderline-angry, which was pretty uncomfortable given the size of my office.

I recall no words of encouragement as I steered the prison through various crises, let alone any praise for progress made. These terms didn't seem to be in his vocabulary. I remember no useful advice or being told any areas in which he thought I could improve my performance. Nor did he show any desire, as far as I am aware, to understand the complexities or sensitivities of the prison. I deduced he extremely disliked being responsible for a woman's establishment.

I felt my card was forever marked after he marched in one morning to find me dandling a new baby. Their proud parent, a member of staff, had brought it in to show us. He gave me a look of distaste as if to say: *"No Governor of mine should be seen doing something like that!"* But he said nothing; he just glared at me. I hastily thrust the infant back at its mother and scurried after him into my office.

I said nothing to anyone in the prison about how difficult my relationship was with the Machine, but I did mention it to a senior colleague that I knew had worked with him, when I met him at a conference. He told me: "If he doesn't like you, you've had it. He does everything he can to drive you out".

Then a mistake was made in the hiring of two members of temporary staff by the personnel department. I wasn't involved with the process but as Governor, of course, I was ultimately responsible. When the mistake was discovered we immediately took mitigating action and I informed the Machine. He berated me both verbally and in his visit report which was submitted to the Director.

He then repeated the bollocking in two subsequent visit reports even though the issue had long been resolved. I felt he was getting some sadistic enjoyment from this. I began to welcome his arrival like I looked forward to root-canal work.

Then the axe fell.

The Machine rang me early one morning at home when I was preparing to leave for work. It had been a tough 24 hours. We had another woman in a medical-induced coma following a suicide attempt.

"Brockhill is going to be re-roled to a male prison" he announced. He sounded triumphant. Stunned, I said nothing. I knew any prison could be re-roled but I had no idea this was on the cards. He continued: "I intend to merge it with xxxx prison. It won't need two in-charge Governors. You can work for xxxx". He announced the name of the person he was putting in charge over me. I spluttered something, tried to ask a question. He put the phone down on me.

I went to work barely able to process what I had heard. At lunchtime, I called a full-staff meeting and broke the news to the troops about the re-role. I was aware that most of them had never worked with male prisoners and some might be anxious about doing so. I tried to sell them the benefits of the change: staff would be dealing with much lower rates of self-harm and suicide. I didn't break the news of the planned merger or the inevitable reduction in staff posts that would follow that.

I was then hit by the next missile. The Prison Inspectorate were enroute for an unannounced inspection.

Then followed days while I attempted to manage the fall out from the announcement, the aftermath of the attempted suicide and the demands of the Inspectorate. The Machine rang me two or three times, issuing curt instructions. He would terminate each call immediately after passing on the information. It was clear to me he wasn't interested in my views on how to manage the forthcoming changes, how the prison was coping, or any concerns I might have about my personal situation.

During this time a very senior manager who had been a friend of mine in years past, and who had been involved in the decision to re-role Brockhill, contacted me to ask how things were. I was glad to hear from him and made a silly joke to my Governors about his part in the proceedings and how I was feeling, which I told him about. It was a stupid joke but I had made it with affection - I was sure he would look out for us. I had made a bad mistake. He was angry, thought me disrespectful, and told me off, saying I could be sacked by saying something like that. This didn't make me feel any better, or any less isolated. I felt I had lost my only ally.

The difficult days continued. Then at last, realisation hit. I was now certain there was no chance that the Machine was ever going to change his mind about me. I saw him continuing to look for any reason to pillory me and the re-role had given him the excellent opportunity to stamp my career into the dust.

This man never swore at me or physically abused me, but I felt unsupported, denigrated and humiliated by him. I know many people have suffered much much worse for much much longer but it wasn't pleasant and I knew I could no longer cope working for him, while trying to keep the prison afloat. Having made a decision, trembling due to the adrenaline flying around my body and the enormity of what I was about to do, I drove home that night and then, my family standing silently by my side, knowing I shouldn't be interrupted, I emailed my union informing them I wanted to make a formal complaint.

A couple of days later a Prison Service Director summoned me to London. He kindly brought me tea and biscuits in the Tate Gallery. I felt incredibly weary but strangely calm. He mentioned that the Machine was due to retire shortly. Then he acknowledged that there had been other concerns about his behaviour and 'management style' over the years. He also claimed, though, that one or two people who had worked for him, did actually speak up in his favour. Sure, I thought cynically, Stockholm Syndrome.

The Director pointed out that if a formal investigation was launched into my complaints the Machine would no doubt come up with counter allegations and it could be embarrassing and damaging for me. I didn't doubt it. I imagined the Machine delighting in describing me as an over-emotional wreck unfit to govern. There was also the tiny matter of whom I would work for during the investigation. My union had requested another line manager be appointed to manage me in the interim, but the Director wouldn't agree to that. The Director suggested we give up on the investigation, and that instead I quit Brockhill to move to a post working for the Women's policy team "*to make use of your experience*". I agreed.

I should probably have fought harder to stay where I was and for the investigation to proceed, but it was a practical decision. I was exhausted.

By going so easily I would be achieving what I was sure the Machine wanted, to get rid of me quickly, which stuck in my craw, but I'd had enough. I just felt an overwhelming sense of relief at that moment, that I would no longer have to deal with him.

Nowadays, the decision to move an alleged victim out of their post without properly investigating their allegations, in preference to inconveniencing someone whose previous behaviour was at least 'suspect', might I think raise a furore. Maybe it would have done so then if it had become known. But I wasn't telling anyone.

I told the staff and my management team that I was going, but not the real reason why. They gave me some lovely gifts and cards. I felt tremendously guilty, particularly when they were facing so much upheaval.

The prison duly re-roled to a male prison causing some furious reaction in the media on behalf of the women who would now face longer journeys to court as well as more difficulty linking up with resettlement services. Some families would also have much further to travel for those, already infrequent, visits. The Inspectorate also strongly disagreed with the decision.

Shortly afterwards, Brockhill was amalgamated into the expansive, newly named HMP Hewell. Not long after that it was deemed uneconomical and closed forever.

The brand new multi-million pound women's healthcare centre, at last completed, was never opened.

Today the prison is inhabited only by rabbits.

Chapter 12: What About The Women?

Industrial Action, Women's Wing HMP Risley, Manchester, 1984

The segregation unit is subterranean and resembles a dungeon. It stinks. I flash my torch through the scratched observation slit as I pass each cell, but it is hard to make out much. I turn a corner. There is a blood-curdling scream right by my ear and I nearly drop the torch. I unlock the hatch on the cell door. The woman is standing there, rigid, white, like a ghost. She is glassy eyed and doesn't seem to see me. I try to reassure her, talking gently, telling her she is safe. She seems to relax a little and eventually I shut the hatch and walk on. But before I have taken three paces the scream repeats. It happens several more times. I reassure her, she relaxes, I walk away and she screams. At last, after what seems like an eternity, she stops screaming. I creep away, leaving her just standing there, still, silent, now departed in her head, somewhere else that I can't imagine.

I return to the wing office and gratefully accept a cup of tea from a colleague also holding the fort during the latest dispute.

I locate the woman's file in the desk. There is a brief entry stating that her baby has been taken by social services. No excuse is given why she is in prison.

Those screams stay with me.

Prison Service HQ, 2004-2012

In the Autumn of 2004 I joined the Prison Service Women's Team and began commuting to Burton-upon-Trent. I was 42. The guilt of leaving those I had grown close to at Brockhill remained like a small stone in my gut.

I couldn't deny that I felt lighter, though. Each morning I would drive for an hour to the pleasant office on the industrial estate, smiling at the countryside, humming along to the radio and basking in the total absence of operational responsibility. No longer wondering how we were going to find staff for that bed watch. No longer dreading 'the' phone call. It was lovely. You could take a lunch break. Visit the shopping centre. Like normal people! Feeling very daring, I signed up for evening classes at the Birmingham School of Acting. My first night climbing the steep steps up to the studio, above the grimy, incongruously named 'Paradise Circus' roundabout, I was in my Seventh Heaven.

The Burton Office alas was not to survive. As part of a national review of the Prison Service estate some months after my arrival, we were ordered to close it. Great was the grief. A couple of staff were lost, and others had to change their roles and were not happy. The few who were unable to commute to London were lodged locally in isolated offices or the Prison Service College. I began commuting to London again, but it wasn't as bad as before. I was in charge of my own diary, could sometimes stay over in a variety of interesting hotels (in one of them I flooded the floor below) and could sometimes, luxury of luxury, work from home.

We were an enthusiastic and I think happy team. It included a mixture of non-operational and operational staff together with a secondee from Prison Health and two psychologists.

I ran a couple of team-building events. One of these was at a very nice hotel in Wellesborne. I tried to impress upon everyone how we, like the crew of Apollo 13 (I made them watch the film) could achieve amazing, life-changing results out of not very much at all. Then we all went home, having caught the Winter Vomiting Bug.

A new Head of the Women's Policy Team was soon to take over. Simon was an able young man, clearly on the way up, but very self-effacing. I liked him immediately. The first thing he set out to do was educate himself about his new responsibilities.

As part of his quest to understand women's prisons, Simon took me with him to HMP&YOI Cornton Vale, then the only women's prison in Scotland. It was facing many of the same issues as we were, including enormous levels of self-injury. They had a high turnover of Governors and I did not envy the new Governor his task, having to meet the needs in a single prison, of everyone from an adult lifer, to a 15 year old on remand. The previous Governor had created a pleasant hostel outside the walls, providing comfortable accommodation where women could live at night, while working in the nearby town. But conditions in much of the rest of the gaol were pretty grim.

I enjoyed my trip with Simon. I got to know him a little and I always craved an opportunity to travel. On the way back when we had an hour between connections at Edinburgh Waverley, I excitedly burst out of the train and ran like an idiot down the Royal Mile looking for souvenirs to buy for the kids. I ended up with one of the millions of tiny toy bagpipes produced for tourists that we would never get to function, and a bag stuffed full of shortbread.

Later Simon's responsibilities were to increase. We looked after children as young as fifteen in our establishments and the Prison Service was suddenly placed in a purchaser/provider relationship with the new Youth Justice Board. Simon was given the job of managing this arrangement and our group expanded in size and was renamed the Women & Young People's Group (W&YPG). Another manager was appointed to lead the Juvenile side and, to reflect the fact that the lead for Women would need to act more independently, my post was upgraded. I applied for the promotion and was successful. This was a significant psychological boost for me after my experience at Brockhill and I was proud to have been trusted with the responsibility of leading the Women's Team.

This change however, did mean the demise of a Prison Service team led by a Senior Civil Servant, whose sole mission had been to champion the cause of women.

Because the Women's 'Estate' had been dissolved, there was little we could now offer

Governors of Women's prisons that was tangible (i.e. a budget) and we had limited powers of persuasion (i.e.we did not line manage them). They had to please new masters now. At least I could empathise with the issues they were struggling with, especially Governors of the local prisons who battled daily to keep their women alive and I did my best to champion their cause whenever I had the opportunity.

I visited all the women's prisons to discover what they were dealing with. Only flashes remain in my mind of this time, like old viewmaster slides: A bat living in the gate-lodge in HMP Foston Hall. A prisoner who liked strangling people, too dangerous to ever think of moving out of a segregation unit. A tiny bird sanctuary at HMP Downview presided over by a proud Officer and a cross owl. The joyful opening of a prison radio station at HMP Styal. A Governor with a worried face who treated us with exceptional deference, serving us tea and sandwiches on bone china plates. I visited HMP Drake Hall on Remembrance

Day and was asked to announce the two minute silence over the radio. As the guns so long ago fell silent on foreign fields, we remembered them. Throughout the prison women stood like statues. It was very moving.

I wrote what I hoped was useful operational advice for Governors. One example was a protocol for the escorting of women who experience miscarriage, terminations, stillbirth or neonatal death. While in Brockhill, I had debriefed two members of staff who had, unprepared and completely inappropriately, been forced to be in the room as a woman underwent a late abortion. What all three women went through was horrific.

The team did retain some specific operational roles. We managed appeals by women who had been refused entry into mother and baby units and assisted the Security Group in their assessment of Restricted Status women (similar to Category A in the male estate). We helped determine these womens' location too, but there was little choice. They either went to the new private prison HMP Bronzefield or HMP Low Newton, which were the only prisons deemed secure enough to hold them.

One of our routine tasks was managing requests from transgender prisoners to transfer into the women's estate. There had been transgender prisoners living in women's prisons for years including one or two lifers. Left to languish in the male estate the lives of transgender prisoners could be beyond hell. There had been an occasional difficulty with this arrangement, but nothing insurmountable.

Gender Recognition Certificates were introduced in 2004 and from that point, when women managed to acquire these to officially recognise their gender there were usually few difficulties. Women would either arrive at our gates straight from court, or occasionally in the early days, they were briefly (and illegally) held in the male estate until they were transferred.

Other prisoners however had lived as women for years, some since childhood, but had not yet acquired a certificate. One of our team would respond to calls from staff in the male estate to visit and interview the woman and the staff who knew her, and assess any risk.

This way we continued to admit a small number of carefully assessed trans women without Gender Recognition Certificates into women's prisons.

With or without GRCs, when trans women arrived staff would often have to manage some nervousness from existing prisoners. Many of our women had experienced violence from men, and some were very fearful of living alongside trans women, even when these women posed no risk to them at all.

When a prisoner had acquired a Gender Recognition Certificate and requested to transfer, we were of course legally obliged to facilitate this. On one occasion in the early days, the Prison Service however, decided to block transfer. This decision was taken at Director General level. This person was a transgender prisoner who had lived as a woman for a number of years. She had been diagnosed as having a dangerous and severe personality disorder and had recently been convicted of raping a woman. The Prison Service argued that she could cope in the male estate, and maintained in the women's estate she would need to be permanently segregated. The judge pointed out correctly that the Women's Estate already had to cater for women who were a severe risk to each other, found in the prisoner's favour, and the move went ahead.

I drafted, I believe, the first policy on the management of transgender and transsexual prisoners in the UK. There was much nervousness at the time and I couldn't get it blessed as an official Prison Service Instruction, however we followed our policy anyway and later it was used as a basis for Prison Service Instruction 07/2011 'the Management of Transexual prisoners'.[16]

---

16 This Policy was superseded on 31 October 2019 by: The Care and Management of Individuals who are Transgender (Ministry of Justice).

While the debate had raged about male to female trans prisoners, we quietly held onto a female to male transgender prisoner, who held a Gender Recognition Certificate, at his own request, rather than transfer him into the male estate. He felt safer in the Women's Estate, too.

I often ended up being dragged into disputes between Governors over which was the best, or more often 'least worst', equipped prison to manage certain women, even though it was now the various Area Managers' job to fight these issues out. The arguments inevitably centred around who had the poorest healthcare facilities.

On one awful occasion a Governor refused entry to a bus carrying a transferring woman after she had been on the road for hours, after the prison doctor declared his health care centre could not cater for her needs.

I would sometimes impotently, appeal to Prison Health representatives in HQ to intervene, or at least offer some useful advice, but they were always singularly unhelpful.

I found Prison Health at these highest echelons intensely annoying. The Heads never ceased to tell me that the way the National Health Service was organised nationally meant no one had any right to interfere in any way operationally with how prison health teams did their business, so they were unwilling to get involved at all. On top of that, I was constantly expected to attend endless erudite health strategy meetings that never seemed to produce any tangible result whatsoever. They just seemed to me to be incredibly expensive talking shops. If I could get out of them, I did.

I found myself frequently lobbied by interest groups and charities for support for their work in women's prisons and also for funding. The latter was pointless as we had none, but we were keen to promote good practice in the prisons, and smooth access into the places, where appropriate.

A lovely woman rang me to say that her charity had printed copies of a beautiful book of illustrated poems, intended as gifts for prisoners, written by women who had experienced self-harm in their lives. After I received a copy I had to explain, causing her some distress, that I could not allow the books into our gaols. Many of the poems had explicit details of the way some women self-injure and there was always a risk of triggering similar behaviour. We paid for a smaller booklet to be produced and distributed containing a few of the poems.

Sometimes my encounters with those wishing to help prisoners did not end even so well. At a resettlement conference I   met an ex offender, Monica Oates, who wanted to set up a home for women at risk of offending. I said something she did not quite like, I can't remember what, but she took exception. Later on, I had some further contact with Ms Oates and did not immediately give her the whole-hearted support she was after. I was cautious about endorsing her project without further investigation, partly because by then I knew the nature of her previous offending, which involved serious financial irregularities. Later I heard Ms Oates had been bad-mouthing me in other forums and slating me on social media. Some time afterwards I discovered that she was in Holloway having been convicted of serious stalking offences.

I remained keen to improve the support that we gave to the children of prisoners.

In 2005 I researched and wrote a guide for Governors and practitioners about what could realistically be provided in terms of family and parental support services in women's prisons. Many women prisoners struggle with their ability to retain any parenting role at all, as they battle addiction, mental health issues and the effects of abuse. It is the duty of all agencies to ensure that where it is in the interests of the child, these links are maintained and the relationship flourishes.

My little book tried to include everything from how to support women to tell their children that they are in custody, through how to provide suitable play areas in visits areas, to appropriate parenting programmes that should be facilitated if resources allow. I received help to produce it from a wide range of people, in particular the great charity KIDS VIP as well as one of the social workers I had worked with in the Thames Valley Partnership.

Beloved Daughter Number One, though, was less than impressed. She snorted in derision when she heard: "You're writing what? A Parenting guide! You two are hopeless parents! You set no boundaries. We do exactly what we like..."

In 2004 parts of the National Probation Service were combined with the Prison Service to form the National Offender Management Service (NOMS). Soon afterwards a national plan was produced designed to reduce reoffending. The plan identified seven 'Pathways to Resettlement' and described how prisoners could be helped with various problems from debt to homelessness.

I set out to determine how these 'pathways' were different, if they were, for women. I also took the opportunity to invent and add a couple more 'pathways', building on my experience at Brockhill. I called these:

Pathway 8: Support for women prisoners who have been abused, raped, or who have experienced domestic violence, and:

Pathway 9: Support for women prisoners who have been involved in prostitution.

Women who had been involved in sex work were barely recognised as a group that existed in the prison system, but they were there, often with multiple needs.

Our *Strategy and Resource Guide* containing these 'pathways' for women was published in Spring 2006. Between 30th October and 10th December that year, five young women who had been involved in the sex industry, were murdered in Ipswich at the hands of a serial killer. Their devastated mothers began to tell their daughters' stories in the media. Their bravery shone a light on what many who are involved in the sex industry endure.

I was very pleased when Baroness Corston in her influential report specifically endorsed our two new 'pathways'.

The Corston Report was commissioned by then Home Office Minister Baroness Scotland in 2006 to review how vulnerable women were being treated in the Criminal Justice system, after six women died in a year at HMP Styal at their own hands. The consultation was wide ranging.

The Report was published in March 2007 and outlined the need for :

'a distinct, radically different, visibly-led, strategic, proportionate, holistic, woman-centred, integrated approach'. It made forty-three recommendations, some of which covered our territory.

Corston's most significant recommendation was that existing women's prisons should be replaced with small multi-functional custodial units phased in over a period of ten years. A token review was set up into this, in which we participated, but it was obvious that this was going nowhere. No one was going to find the money to replace all women's prisons, even if the population was cut in half by diverting the rest to more appropriate community punishment.

The report also called for general conditions to be improved in prisons. The newly formed Ministry of Justice responded by pointing to the new *Gender Specific Standards* I was at that very moment drafting.

We had begun work on the *Gender Specific Standards* soon after I joined the team. No one told us to do this, we just knew we had to develop a comprehensive set of mandatory standards detailing every single way women prisoners should be treated differently to men according to their needs.

Members of our team had learned much over the years, but now we were touring the country visiting prisons and talking to staff, prisoners, unions and interest groups. Then I wrote the thing.

I managed to get in some fine detail that I thought was important. To give one example:

'Unless they have been placed on 'closed' visits, women should be allowed to hug family and hold young children on their laps if they wish during the visit. Staff and prisoners must be in no doubt about this. Any instance of a child being used to pass contraband should be referred as a safeguarding (child protection) concern.'

It seems incredible that this would need to be written, but there were reasons for it. Staff at at least one prison had been preventing women from holding their toddlers and babies brought in to visit them, due to fear that they might be used by their visitors to pass them drugs. This was even after both the children and the visitors had been searched. The staff in good faith were trying to do what they thought was right. The very real threat of potentially lethal drugs entering prisons however, has to be managed against the needs of the prisoner, and more importantly, the needs of the young child. The Governor of one of the prisons where staff were stopping women holding their babies and toddlers incidentally, was completely unaware that it was happening. Often much pain is inflicted due to a lack of leadership, or supervision, or the rules not being clear.

Another auditable standard included was:

'Staff and managers are aware that women prisoners are unlikely to make formal complaints and (must) seek other means of feedback'

We had learned that women prisoners were less likely than their male counterparts to make formal complaints about anything. They would seek to resolve issues informally straight away, and only then if they had staff around them that they trusted. Foreign nationals were the least likely to complain of all, fearing repercussions for their immigration status.

One more standard cemented an existing 'protocol'. It concerned an issue that had badly tripped up a previous Minister, the Rt Hon Ann Widdecombe, when she had attempted to defend the indefensible:

'Pregnant women are not handcuffed after arrival at a hospital or clinic. Women in labour are not handcuffed either en route to, or while in hospital. Restraints are carried but not applied unless necessary.'

In 1995 it had been revealed that women in labour were being handcuffed and then chained on what are called 'closetting chains,' right up to the point of actually giving birth and then immediately after the birth. Channel 4 News had broadcast secretly-filmed footage of a heavily pregnant woman in chains at the Whittington Hospital in London.

Presenting *Prison Service Order 4800 Women Prisoners* containing the *Gender Specific Standards* to the massed ranks of Heads of Group and Directors for sign off, was intimidating. It undoubtedly helped that it was so long that no one except the extremely dedicated would have read it. There was one short question and then it passed. We were over the moon. Now women's prisons had standards as baselines for everything that they did and could use them when making plans and competing for resources.

Baroness Corston also recommended in her report that: '...strip searching' in women's prisons should be reduced to the 'absolute minimum compatible with security',

We had already taken on the daunting and controversial task of attempting to prove to the Prison Service that we could safely remove the routine 'strip' search (properly called the 'full' search) of women. I had no doubt that this would be our biggest challenge, and I wasn't sure whether we could bring it off.

Prison rules stated at this time that every prisoner must be routinely full searched. The argument against conducting so many of these searches particularly on women, was gaining momentum not just within the pressure groups but also within women's prisons.

The full search risks retraumatising people who have been sexually abused. However professionally conducted, it is inevitably an embarrassing and humiliating process. In addition, many women would be menstruating, pregnant or may even have just given birth.

Critically, the usefulness of a *routine* full search (as opposed to an 'on suspicion' full search) was in any event highly suspect. We knew plenty of drugs were being brought into prisons, but we believed women when they knew they were coming into prison, would simply secrete their contraband where we could never discover it, within their own bodies.

Prison staff in the UK do not have the legal power to carry out 'body cavity' searches. In male prisons, men however, may be asked to 'squat'. The purpose of this is to encourage items concealed in the anal passage to emerge. In addition, in a few high security prisons men may be asked to sit on a special chair that should detect metal objects secreted inside them. Neither of these measures have ever been considered a realistic solution to stop drugs coming into women's prisons.

We set out to consult.

We toured the country talking to staff, women prisoners and unions. The only person who remembered finding anything during a routine full search recalled that, on a single occasion, they had found some drugs in a woman's outer clothing.

It was commonly agreed that a woman prisoner would hide what she wanted to hide internally. A nurse that I met reeled off a list of items that, on one occasion, a woman had asked her help to retrieve:

a mars bar

a cheese sandwich

a bottle of Worcester sauce

a pair of taps

I was part of a delegation to Northern Ireland during this time and took the opportunity to visit a women's prison and ask staff's views on the routine full search. Conditions on the wings were austere. The toilets in the rooms flushed regularly and continually and I was told that this was an anti-drugs measure. It would have driven me mad. There was one paramilitary prisoner there but the rest were serving an assortment of medium to short sentences and some were on remand. Whatever the conditions on the wings the women were chatty and relaxed and I was easily manipulated by a canny prisoner in the prison shop into buying an ugly and expensive red wooden cat that she had made. Most of the supervising staff we met were male. I discussed our plans. The staff were astonished and unsympathetic. I was told by senior staff that removing the routine full search would be inconceivable in Northern Ireland. It was a different ballpark of course. During the trip I met a Senior

Officer whose close colleague had been blown up by the IRA.

We got our ducks in a row. We completely accepted that at times there would be a need to full search a woman 'on suspicion'. This needed to be done, for instance, when someone was caught in the act of stealing something and then suspected of hiding it in her underwear, and we designed a new authority and detailed process for that.

We went to Security Group braced for a fight, but to my surprise we didn't get it. In retrospect, we did outnumber them and we were absolutely determined. We may have appeared quite intimidating: they did look a bit shell-shocked.

I went to the Director General to tell him where we had got to. I explained to him that I thought we should be prepared to concede to the retention of routine full searching for Restricted Status and Cat E[17] prisoners. There was no logical reason to full

17 'E' list prisoners are prisoners who are deemed likely to attempt to escape. They have to wear a distinctive uniform when out of their cell.

search these women routinely either, but I thought this might be for some people a 'bridge too far'. He, however, was great. "No", he said. "We should go for the lot".

We trialled the new procedures in three prisons: the changes didn't cause a ripple.

I enjoyed writing the Ministerial Brief. I suspect it's the only time any Minister has ever received a document containing the word 'vaginally'. No objections were raised.

I drafted the Prison Service Instruction and Press Release. I was amazed by the tiny number of objections raised by Prison Service Heads as this historic change was put before them. Clearly the strategy of using the word 'vagina' throughout the documentation continued to work like a charm. I doubt many read below the first paragraph.

Then came the day that the routine full searching of women prisoners ceased. What was achieved was very significant and I am proud to think that I had a major hand in it. The kids said it would be a strange epitaph to put on my gravestone but we should probably do it. I wouldn't mind at all.

As a postscript to this, in 2019 four inmates including a transgender prisoner, were to sue Sodexo (then running HMP Peterborough) and the Ministry of Justice for failing to follow the searching instructions we had so painstakingly written. They won.

Our next major task was to do something about improving training for staff working with women prisoners. At that time there was no specialised training of any kind.

We made the case to the DG and he gave us the resources to enable us to recruit two Senior Prison Officers to develop and deliver a new training package to cover all the different aspects of working in a women's prison. The programme prepared staff for working with women by helping them understand how the lives our women had led, impacted on their emotions, behaviour and risk. The course covered the practical ways staff could best operate, and the emotional impact on them too, of working in such an environment. We called it WASP, the Women's Awareness Staff Programme.

During the development of the programme, the trainers met many different people involved in the supervision and support of women offenders and those at risk of offending. Following a few requests they then developed and began offering a well-received modified version of the course outside the prisons including within the Womens' Centres.[18] We named it 'WASP - In the Community'. Not content to rest on their laurels they then developed a specialised course, 'Sex Workers in Custody and Community' (SWICC).

I attended a course delivered in a Woman's Centre in Birmingham. It was great to see everyone pooling their experience and the skill

---

18 A number of Women's Centres exist throughout the UK and survive precariously on a mixture of public and charitable funding. They are a 'one-stop-shops' providing a range of support for women from drug services through housing advice to counselling for those who have experienced sexual and domestic violence. Some of these women may be ex-offenders or at risk of offending.

displayed by our trainers. These Senior Officers were absolute gems.

We bought a bushel of furry bees to give away on the courses. Strangely enough, you cannot buy cuddly wasps.

There had been criticism by the interest groups for some time about how women prisoners were being transported, with good reason. The movement of women in the same vehicles as men was highly undesirable. The men would soon discover that there was a woman on board and would often make her life a misery, subjecting her to catcalls and abuse - tremendously distressing to someone with mental health problems, or those who had experienced violence.

I lobbied hard for separate transport but I didn't succeed. No one was going to pay for it. A 'compromise' was provided. As vehicles were redesigned, suppliers, in conjunction with the Prison Escort Contract Service, built vans with a separate entrance through which, in theory, women would be able to enter without being spotted by the men. Now all they had to do was keep silent. How many times have women heard that down the ages?

One of our main challenges in the team was to try and encourage Governors to commission appropriate therapeutic interventions for their women. This was why we had psychologists in the team. It was no easy task.

One of our difficulties was of course our total lack of any funding to give Governors to make it happen. They needed somehow to find the money themselves, if they wanted to run programmes.

There were other problems. Most programmes, where they had been tried, had been 'genderised.' In other words, programmes designed for men had in some way been tweaked to try to make them more 'feminine'. There was very little evidence even then that they would work with women, as the numbers of participants involved in most programmes were simply too small to evaluate.

We knew some things. We knew that abuse and early traumatic life experiences led women to unhealthy coping strategies (like drug-taking) which often led to offending. We knew that women were at slightly lower risk of reoffending than men but when they did reoffend, they would often be convicted of multiple offences, usually of a less serious nature.

Sue Kennedy, a senior psychologist in our team, was working on something entirely new. This was the holy grail. Choices, Actions, Relationships and Emotions (CARE) was designed as a programme for adult women with a history of violence and complex needs and a medium to high risk of reconviction. Throughout almost my entire time in HQ, Sue diligently worked on this programme. Even before it was accredited, it had won awards and it was endorsed in the Corston report. I was greatly exercised, however, by the time the Service was taking to get it accredited and off the ground and deeply worried whether we would ever manage to persuade anyone to fund it. Luckily, eventually, the newly formed NOMS Interventions Group galloped in like King Arthur and his knights to provide the organisational muscle needed, and it ran a couple of times before I left.

The issue of how we treat female sex offenders was also always on our minds. There was no equivalent to the male Sex Offender Treatment Programme in the women's estate. There were small numbers of women sex offenders in the system, but many more than people realised. In complete contrast to the men, their presence was tolerated and the effects of their behaviour minimised both in prison, and in wider society. They were not being challenged about the damage inflicted on their victims and some of them remained very much a risk. This was one of the areas of work our Principal Psychologist, Caroline Stewart, headed up and she supported the Lucy Faithfull Foundation as they developed an individual tool for working with the women, but no long term funding was forthcoming from anywhere for individual therapeutic intervention. The numbers continued to build.

Corston had recommended that a civil servant with sole responsibility for women offenders be appointed at '*very senior - director level*' who would ensure progress. That did not happen. I was still to be the most senior civil servant with sole responsibility for women. A Ministerial Champion for Women and Criminal Justice however was appointed: Maria Eagle Labour MP at the Ministry of Justice.

I was wary of working with politicians.

Down the years I had seen the consequences of political interference with the Prison Service. Initiatives had been forced upon us requiring vast amounts of work and cost to implement, yet most of us in prisons knew they were doomed to failure, particularly without the ongoing resources necessary to sustain them.

One classic political initiative was 'Intermittent Custody' which saw low risk prisoners sentenced to a 'weekend in prison', expected to travel halfway across the country, spending most of their time while there, being received into custody, assessed, inducted, then processed again for release. Meanwhile, managers would be scratching their heads wondering how to keep cells empty for their arrival when spaces were always at such a premium.

The most disastrous initiative by far however, was the introduction of '*Indeterminate Sentences for Public Protection*' (IPP). These were brought in by the Labour Government in 2003 for offenders who were deemed to pose a danger to the public but had not yet committed crimes that qualified for a Life Sentence. Intended to protect the public, this change in the law sentenced thousands of prisoners, many of them young, to indefinite incarceration and, without any of the necessary interventions in place that would enable them to address their underlying issues, left them without any realistic prospect of release. Over time the behaviour and mental health of many would deteriorate and applications for parole would fail. The injustice of the system was finally recognised and the IPP sentence was abolished in 2012. Thousands of prisoners with the sentence however continue to languish in prison to this day unable to convince any parole board that they will be able to cope living independently without committing further offences.[19]

There are no votes in improving conditions for prisoners but politicians have often seen political opportunity in eviscerating them. Most initiatives I saw were blatantly designed to demonstrate to the public how 'tough' the current government was. Sudden announcements of draconian prison 'reforms' would enthusiastically be announced in the right wing press: of cutting temporary release schemes, of restricting parole, of increasing the length of sentences. Urgent secret messages would be sent to Governors from Prison Service HQ warning us of expected prisoner unrest, self

---

19 As of November 2019 there were still 2,223 people in prison serving an IPP sentence and a further 1,203 who had been released but had been recalled to prison. (Ministry of Justice).

harm and suicide. Typically, announcements would result in a rapid increase in numbers of prisoners in custody. Prisoners would be 'doubled up' or even' 'trebled up' in tiny Victorian cells meant for one. Portacabins would be flown over prison walls and installed on exercise yards. Ancient crumbling cells that had been decommissioned would be brought back into use. In 1997 HMP Weare, an actual ship, was commissioned and moored off Portland to house 400 prisoners. The Victorian Prison Hulks lived again. Several times all prisons were full to bursting and police cells began filling up costing way more in police overtime than it would ever have cost to keep prisoners in prison. At one point a Minister stood up in Parliament and declared: *"We no longer have prisoners in police cells"*. It was technically correct, but at the same time, I was told, there was a bus load of prisoners in a cellular van circling the M25.

And when things went wrong not because of mismanagement but of a genuine lack of resources, or because of a sudden switch of political priorities, Governors, or occasionally the then Director General, would always be firmly lobbed the can. Whenever there was a Government reshuffle Prison Service leads would brace themselves to see who would inherit the job of Prisons Minister. Surely, second to Northern Ireland, the poisoned chalice of any Government.

For the first time now, however, there was genuine political interest in improving the lot of one small group of vulnerable prisoners - women.

I thought my first meeting with Maria Eagle went well. I had been summoned to answer some questions and we met in one of the boardrooms in the House of Commons. Much varnished wood and red velvet was in evidence. Afterwards, the mainstream civil servant accompanying me politely and definitively told me off. "We were not there to brief the Minister!" she said. Weren't we? I had, unprompted, expressed cynicism after Maria Eagle remarked that female magistrates were likely to be more compassionate towards the women before them, than their male counterparts. I knew different: they were far harsher.

The Minister was determined to make a difference. She appeared suspicious of most civil servants whom she didn't think shared her determination to make the Corston dream more than just another report. I felt, however, that she judged our little team was doing the best we could, and she summoned me back to her office several times. I was impressed by her stubbornness: she didn't give up easily. She managed to secure more than £14 million out of the Treasury for the Women's Centres to divert vulnerable women at risk, away from offending.

Now I was spending much of my time writing Ministerial briefings. If it wasn't about progress, or the lack of it, on Corston, it was about what women prisoners were up to. Women's prisons were a source of endless media interest. Questions were always being asked in parliament.

One scary morning the Minister summoned me to sit in the Chamber in the House of Commons to feed her answers while she was being grilled. I was crammed into the wooden civil servants' 'box', with a few others, at the front of the Chamber on the government side, horribly visible to spectators. The seat, designed no doubt to stop you nodding off, was hard. There were quite a few MPs present on the green leather benches, or milling in and out.

The ex Chief Inspector of Prisons Ramsbotham began the debate and set the tone by speaking about the time that he had walked out of Holloway, he had been so appalled at the conditions. Particularly the cockroaches.

My difficulty wasn't thinking of suggested responses to the questions, but my handwriting, which is never good at the best of times. I scribbled three versions of each suggested answer, to ensure at least one was legible.

I was now representing women offenders in all NOMS meetings. I was still usually the only woman there.

For hours I would sit in rectangular grey meeting rooms, windows sealed fast lest the pigeons hop in, or someone else think "enough is enough" and hop out. On the rectangular table would be boiled sweets and lime juice, which no one ever touched. Men would sit round in rectangular grey suits, pretending to have read the sheaf of paper in front of them. A couple of them would be leaning back on their chairs, fancying themselves the rebels of the floor in slightly louder ties. And looking out of place, and slightly less rectangular, me. Inevitably my moment would come. Those engaged in polite discussions (or tense arguments) about some new policy or change designed to meet the needs of men would eventually, briefly, draw breath and I would leap in with my well practised sweet smile to demand piercingly and annoyingly: "But what about the Women?!"

Gradually at last though, they were learning to anticipate the question. The Equality Act had become law and after 2010 everyone suddenly had to wrestle with writing *Equality Impact*

Assessments. These required agencies to consider the impact of their policies on different groups of people affected - one of those groups being women. We assisted with these whenever anyone would let us and had hopes that this would result in more equality for women offenders within the system.

I found myself increasingly required to turn up at conferences to give talks about women offenders. I did not enjoy this. I never really like speaking as 'myself'. Moveover this was in the early days of Powerpoint and inevitably the technology would fall apart which I never knew how to fix. I learned to carry a sheaf of papers and be prepared to improvise, mourning the loss of the overhead projector and dry wipe pens that I understood.

Those I never minded talking to however, were members of the judiciary.

I was particularly keen to communicate the reality of what life was like in prisons to those who sent our women there. In her report, Corston had recommended: *'Women must never be sent to prison for their own good, to teach them a lesson, for their own safety, or to access services such as detoxification'*.

Time and again it was clear that this was exactly what was happening. 16% of women prisoners had no previous convictions compared to only 9% of men. A Judge told me that on principle he would remand a woman for two weeks to get her off drugs and stabilised, and then bring her back to sentence her. He seemed to have never heard of bail schemes. The magistracy in particular felt that they had no alternative option to custody and often saw prison as a *'place of safety'*.

In my talks I made sure I included the self-injury statistics.

I found myself the representative for women offenders on a European Social Fund working group. This involved some long journeys to meetings and much assessment of bids as prisons, probation teams and other bodies vied for a slice of European money to develop innovative ways to tackle offending. Some schemes broke new ground and brought new money into the system which was useful, as was some sharing of best practice across Europe.

I was invited to conferences on the back of this, in Berlin and Budapest. I remember nothing alas about the work we did in Berlin. I know that my group ended up confusingly booking into the wrong hotel in Potsdam. I also recall sitting through a very long lecture in German in Berlin, before discovering that I had been provided with a headset offering simultaneous translation. The only other memory I have is of slipping out one lunchtime. I wandered up towards the Brandenburg Gate and found myself surrounded by the grey grasping monoliths of the holocaust memorial. I was drawn in and down and overwhelmed, as the architects no doubt intended.

Likewise, I don't recall anything at all about the discussions I had with colleagues in Budapest. There was an exceptional vegetarian meal, a colourful market, and a tour of the two cities. We also visited the Dohány Street Synagogue where we viewed the precious vessels and menorah that loving and desperate guardians had somehow saved from the holocaust. There was a trip to the steam baths. As I relaxed in the warm water under the stars, idly wondering why I was the only woman in a pool of very fed Budapestian men, I reflected on how lucky I was to have these opportunities.

I also thought about my current position. I now seemed to be permanently stuck in HQ. It wasn't my favourite place. I missed the cut and thrust of a prison. Neither could I see myself being promoted any higher into the Senior Civil Service. Whether or not, of course, I actually had the ability to go further, I didn't think I was a natural fit. For one thing I would hate having to be obsequious to Ministers if I was ever to be put in a position where I strongly disagreed with them. I also thought I would have other problems. I never enjoyed 'networking' and that seemed to be a major part of the average Senior Civil Servant's day. Also, many SCS I knew seemed to be ultra confident, skilled at advancing their own position, and that I knew I would never be. I had a hard enough time 'selling myself' on selection boards. Maybe part of me was still that self-conscious introverted little girl, whose mother would behave bizarrely in public or scream after her down the street. I am the classic actor who is only truly comfortable attracting attention when being someone else.

In that pool in Budapest however, I was content with what I had achieved. It was what I had always wanted: to become independent, to earn a good living, to find a family and occasionally to be able to stand up for the underdog. Although many times I would be angry, frustrated and cynical about how the Prison Service was run, I would be everlastingly grateful for the opportunities I had.

I returned home thankful for the brief break from HQ, and ready to get down to work again.

In May 2010 the Labour Government fell and the Cameron-Clegg coalition took power and introduced new austerity measures, the most severe this country has seen since the Second World War. The pressure on the National Offender Management Service to reduce costs became extreme.

The women's prisons were easy targets.

Corston had recommended that systematic safeguards be put in place if a prison closed, so that good practice approaches, like Carousel, would not be lost. She had been impressed by our innovative programme at Brockhill. Accurately, and slightly painfully for me, however, she pointed out that the Women and Young People's Group had no money and little influence to ensure its rescue. The Ministry of Justice in response had given no reassurances that Carousel would be saved but assured her that in the event of any future loss of 'nationally important provision', W&YPG would '*work with partners, intervening at the appropriate level to achieve this*'. No problem there then.

Following Brockhill, HMP Bullwood Hall in Essex had been re-roled to a male prison in 2006 and it was suddenly announced that HMP Send in Woking would be the next. Send prison contained our only therapeutic community for women. We hastily researched the implications of moving the facility to HMP Downview in Surrey, our next nearest prison. It wouldn't be straightforward. For starters, a new specialist health provider would have to be commissioned to oversee the therapy: the prisons fell under different health providers, which would not help matters. Next, to run the community additional Prison Officers would have to be recruited and trained at Downview. As a serious added complication, Downview did not then take lifers, and as those women were the main clients for the community, we would need this to change. Lifers would inevitably mean a slightly more hard-core population and would probably necessitate a security upgrade to the prison and the money for that would have to be found. Downview staff were aware of what was being discussed and the Prison Officers Association looked likely to be resistant.

To manage all the changes, the therapeutic community would have to be closed for many months, with negative consequences for our women. And while all this was going on we were going to have to deal with inevitable flak from the media and pressure groups. The debate raged between us, the Governors of the two establishments, NOMS Leads and Estate Planning Group for weeks.

The therapeutic community still flourishes in Send women's prison.

Other prisons did fall. The opening of privately owned HMP Bronzefield and HMP Peterborough had provided the necessary capacity for it to happen. HMP Morton Hall was next, sold off to become an Immigration Removal Centre in 2011. Many women's prisons were neither ideally located nor situated, however any loss of accommodation meant prisoners uprooted. When a closure or re-role was announced, the Women's Team would hot-foot it to the prison and, while commiserating with the shell-shocked staff, begin interviewing and working out what to do with often distressed women.

Eventually it was announced that the two beautiful stately homes masquerading as women's Open Prisons were to close. Logically speaking, their location didn't make any sense, lying many miles from most women's home areas. However some excellent resettlement work was taking place and they had great community support. HMP&YOI Askham Grange had an innovative children's day care centre serving the community as well as the residents, and had developed a productive relationship with Timpson's to train women. Moreover, HMP&YOI East Sutton Park had just featured on The Apprentice - a team had dropped in to buy some sausages from the farm! Swathes of distress swept the gaols, the press had a field day and the pressure groups gave NOMS a major roasting.

The prisons ended up temporarily reprieved but the Sword of Damocles continued to hang over them.

The problems of running the ill-designed Holloway continued and the economic benefits of selling the real estate became increasingly attractive. After I left the Prison Service, stabilisation in the overall number of women prisoners was to enable its closure. This was hailed by many as a triumph, given its dark and often controversial history. However its passing was mourned by staff and many 'regulars' who had regarded it as home.

Our little battles continued. Much bigger ones were being fought outside our corridors.

At last the numbers of women in prison were reducing.

Conditions in prisons, despite the pressure on everyone to reduce costs, were improving.

Most wonderfully, the number of self-inflicted deaths in women's prisons was falling. In the eight years between 2005 and 2013 there were 25 deaths, which is a terrible figure, but in 2004 <u>alone</u> there had been 13. The statistics masked of course the fact that staff in our prisons continued to save dozens of lives every day, through preventative care and catching 'near misses'. The shock and terror on the faces of those staff at Brockhill would never leave me.

The drive to cut costs continued. The fruit that had been introduced into meetings throughout government to promote health (but rarely eaten), disappeared. Times were clearly desperate! Cleland House was shut and everyone was moved to open plan offices in Clive House, Petty France and fought for a desk each morning. Lest we worried about having to work next to someone who was too loud or otherwise offensive, each team was advised to nominate a 'village elder' to keep the peace. Within our team the suggested person, who was in her fifties, was more than a little offended. We knuckled down. We might have no space to work and the photocopiers always seemed to be out of order but there was a very nice coffee stand on the ground floor. I discovered Chai Latte.

My boss Simon, with whom I had worked so well, much to my regret announced that he was leaving to lead the new, soon to be infamous, 'Specifications, Benchmarking and Costings' team. This team was tasked with enabling public sector prisons to compete with the private sector and would end up drastically reducing operational staff within English and Welsh prisons. The dramatic reduction of staff together with an unexpected tsunami of new and lethal street drugs coming into prisons, wreaked devastation throughout the Service. Assaults, self-injuries and suicides rocketed. But that was to come.

Chapter 13: End of My Era

Stratford upon Avon Summer 2014

"And what did you do before you retired?" The cheerful young woman pouring my tea has clearly labelled me as one of the no longer gainfully employed.

I put down the play I have been reading and shuffle in my seat. Sometimes I choose not to answer that question properly, hiding behind the label of 'Civil Servant'. But today I do: "I was a Prison Governor". Her eyes widen in shock. Then comes the inevitable rhetorical question:

"That must have been terribly hard work." I pause for a second, thinking of some of the jobs other people have to do.

"It had its moments".

"I bet you're glad you've retired."

"Yes...but I miss the people".

Prison Service HQ Clive House

2012-2013

The hit came on HQ first. A third of jobs were to go in a brutal restructure. As managers we tried to reassure our teams but we had no control over what was happening. All I could promise them was that I would tell them all I knew, as soon as I was able to do so. It was pretty heartbreaking. We could envision so much of the innovative work we had done being undone and the lessons we had learned being forgotten.

Then it was announced that the Women's Team was about to be subsumed into the existing 'Equalities Group'.

Only a few years before there had been a separately managed Women's Estate, now the needs of women were to be represented in a mere subset. I had few illusions how little time this group would have to focus on women's needs. It wasn't like the Equalities' agenda was exactly small. They had a few things on their plate (recruitment, training, promotions, investigations, public relations...) As a somewhat feeble attempt to deflect the inevitable criticism, it was decided that the new group would be titled: 'Women and Equalities Group', not the other way round. To indicate that women would not be an afterthought. I managed a wry smile when I heard.

Despite my reservations about entering the Senior Civil Service I applied for the position of Head of the new Group. It would have been a promotion and a major challenge, but I would have given it my all. The Equalities agenda is important to me and my heart leapt for a moment with excitement. I sat the board but wasn't selected. Unfortunately I didn't really take to the successful candidate and I don't think this was just because I was feeling rejected. This person was well regarded because of their academic qualifications, but I found them brusque and they had a tendency to name drop which always irritates me. My precious team was about to be decimated. I feared the Academic would not have the sensitivity, or care enough about my team or appreciate all that they had achieved, to help them through the inevitable pain ahead.

One morning a couple of weeks later, the Academic greeted me with the announcement that, of the two Women's Team trainers, who had designed and delivered our unique training courses all over the country, one had to go. They would have to compete against each other to keep delivering the programmes they had created together.

I reacted impulsively by saying that I wouldn't be able to choose between them, and the Academic would need to chair the selection board. But I lied. I just didn't want to. A displaced trainer from another group also applied for the job which, someone had decided, should be advertised. To my horror, at the board, the Academic picked them.

When I found out I marched up to the Academic's desk and railed at them. They said something about the external candidate "presenting better". I was furious. In my eyes the Academic should not have been more impressed by a slightly slicker presentation, than by the eons of knowledge and understanding our trainers had acquired developing their programmes. The Academic then pointed out that I could have prevented this by not ducking out of chairing the board. This was of course correct. Mortified, I went and apologised abjectly to my sad trainers. They were very kind. Then, always the professionals, while trying to find other posts, they began to train up their successor.

Weeks later, I was stunned to receive a call from the external candidate to say she had decided she didn't want the job after all. One of our trainers was already on her way back to a prison. The other agreed to stay and was, of course, to do a sterling and professional job as she always had done. In her place I'm not sure my heart would have been in it.

My position was now up for evaluation. I had the task of defining what I had actually been doing within the group, to compare with my proposed role in the new structure. Completing the evaluation I successfully, and completely unintentionally, managed to write myself out of a job.

The Academic called me in and informed me that it was clear from what I had written that I had been operating as de-facto Head of Group, which was their job now. As what I had been doing did not match my potential post in the new structure, I would have to compete for the new post if I wanted it, and I would need to be prepared to undertake a significantly reduced role. The Academic added nicely, but I'm sure insincerely, that they hoped I would apply. I told them truthfully that I was glad that I now had options, but I did not want the new position and I would not be applying. I am sure they were as relieved as I was.

I now had two choices: to apply for other posts or to take the early retirement package being offered. Then as a Civil Servant, as I was coming up to my fiftieth birthday I was in the very fortunate position of being able to take my pension, if I chose to go.

One of the few jobs at my grade that was available was in Security Group and I applied, encouraged by fond memories of Woodhill. I sat the selection board but didn't get the job.

I would have considered any post going but nothing was on the horizon. I had the option of hanging around indefinitely, forcing the Service to scrape me up something to do: we were very lucky, no one was being made compulsorily redundant. But I absolutely hated the idea of that: I have never been good at kicking my heels. I agonised for several weeks. It felt so wrong to give up a good salary when we had teenagers to support but this was an opportunity. There were things I knew I wanted to do. I talked it over at length with Rob. My husband, as always, was his logical, reassuring self. He chuckled at my angst. "It sounds like a pretty obvious choice". He said.

In limbo, pending my exit from the Service, I was given an investigation and a short project to complete for the local Area Manager. With excess time on my hands, I painted the dining room, we rescued a ridiculously large dog and I applied to join the Samaritans.

Normally when someone retires from the Service it is a time of excitement and looking forward. Parties are held and speeches are made. No staff preparing to leave in these days however, were 'gate happy'. We were being shunted out fast, and en masse. Many colleagues just slipped away and we soon lost track of those who had already gone. We couldn't complain, we were so much better off than so many other people losing their jobs at that time. Leaving was undoubtedly the best decision for me and possibly put years on my life. At the time, though, it didn't feel like that: it felt like a bereavement.

I wanted to go somewhere peaceful to mark my departure, with those of my team that still remained. We caught a ferry down the Thames to Greenwich, ate chocolate eclairs in a coffee shop and in the late morning sun, climbed the hill to the Observatory. I looked carefully, but any astronomer mice at work were keeping discreetly out of sight.

A few weeks later I returned to London to hand back my laptop and security pass. I saw no one I knew and I didn't seek anyone out. I didn't belong anymore. Rather than catching the train straight home, I walked down Tothill Street, past Westminster Abbey, crossed the Thames and spent the afternoon in Sea World. There I became lost in colour. I went home happy.

Afterword

2021

I have written this book during the Pandemic. I recently had occasion to visit the A&E department at the Alexandra Hospital in Redditch. There I came across a young woman and a young man, both Prison Officers, the man handcuffed to the prisoner by his side. They all waited patiently and quietly before filing into the tiny triage room together. Not for any of them, the luxury of social distancing. Watching, I felt a stab of pride to have been a member of this same Prison Service.

It has been a joy remembering.

ABOUT THE AUTHOR

Barbara was born in 1962 and grew up as an only child in Brighton Sussex. In 1983 she gained a BSc(Econ) at Aberystwyth university in International Politics and Political Science before joining the Prison Service as a trainee Assistant Governor. As part of her training she served a year as a Prison Officer at HMP Holloway. As a Governor grade she worked at HMP Lewes, HMP Wormwood Scrubs, HMYOI Aylesbury and HMP Woodhill and was appointed Governor of HMP Brockhill in 2002. Along the way she worked as Staff Officer to a Prison Service Area Manager and was seconded to the Thames Valley Partnership - a crime reduction charity. In 2005 she was appointed Head of the Women's Team for the Prison Service. She retired from the Prison Service in 2013. Barbara now works in schools providing exam support and is a jobbing professional actor. She is married to Robert and they live in Warwickshire. They have two daughters and an unfeasibly large dog.

Printed in Great Britain
by Amazon

39154980R00205